WORKS ISSUED BY
THE HAKLUYT SOCIETY

PIETER VAN DEN BROECKE'S
JOURNAL OF VOYAGES TO
CAPE VERDE, GUINEA AND ANGOLA
(1605–1612)

THIRD SERIES
NO. 5

Pieter van den Broecke by Frans Hals
The Iveagh Bequest, Kenwood (English Heritage), London

PIETER VAN DEN BROECKE'S JOURNAL OF VOYAGES TO CAPE VERDE, GUINEA AND ANGOLA (1605–1612)

Translated and edited by

J. D. LA FLEUR

THE HAKLUYT SOCIETY
LONDON
2000

Published by The Hakluyt Society
c/o Map Library
British Library, 96 Euston Road,
London NW1 2DB

SERIES EDITORS
W. F. RYAN
ROBIN LAW

ISBN 0 904180 68 9
ISSN 0072 9396

British Library Cataloguing-in-Publication Data
A catalogue record for this book is
available from the British Library

Typeset by Waveney Typesetters, Wymondham, Norfolk
Printed in Great Britain at
the University Press, Cambridge

CONTENTS

ILLUSTRATIONS

MAPS

PREFATORY NOTE

PIETER VAN DEN BROECKE'S MANUSCRIPT

Pieter van den Broecke (1585–1640) wrote a detailed account of four trading journeys which he undertook to western Africa and an extended trip to Arabia, India and the East Indies. He probably composed this account some time after his return to the Netherlands from these voyages in 1630. His account is preserved in a manuscript, which describes his experiences and recollections in the format of a contemporaneously kept daily log-book. This manuscript (MS Leiden, University Library, BPL 952) was the basis for two nearly identical books printed in Haarlem and Amsterdam in 1634. These books, however, presented a highly abridged and significantly altered version of what Van den Broecke had written in his manuscript. Published versions of Van den Broecke's journal were quickly reprinted, adapted, translated, and included in several European encyclopaedic geographies of the seventeenth and eighteenth centuries. For these geographies, Van den Broecke's published accounts constituted an important source, because he was among the earliest of Europeans to describe publicly in detail the communities he encountered in West Africa and Central Africa, and to detail the sophisticated commercial strategies of Dutch merchants then trading on the Atlantic coast of Africa.

In more recent times, scholarly interest in the early history of Africa and the origins of European commercial expansion has made Van den Broecke's account a valuable historical resource. This modern interest supported the publishing of a transliteration of the original manuscript copy of Van den Broecke's African travels in 1950 by the Linschoten Vereeniging, the Dutch historical society for overseas exploration. But the difficulty of reading Van den Broecke's early seventeenth-century Dutch text has caused his manuscript to be, at worst, a source to be ignored or, at best, a difficult source for historians to interpret with adequate accuracy and confidence.

The present edition offers for the first time an English translation of those parts of Van den Broecke's original manuscript which describe his trading voyages to Africa, and provides full Africanist annotation and editorial criticism.

PREFACE

This publication presents an interpretation of parts of a manuscript in Dutch written by Pieter van den Broecke around 1630 (MS Leiden, University Library, BPL 952), which records the multiple trading voyages he made to Africa and the East Indies in the early years of the seventeenth century. Interpreting and transforming his record by editing it, translating it into languages other than Dutch, and reading it in the light of other, similar sources is certainly not a new endeavour.

Van den Broecke, the original author, appears to have been himself engaged in re-working the document prior to its first publication by two different presses in 1634, the first in Haarlem, the second soon after in Amsterdam.[1] By the mid-seventeenth century the editor of a large compilation of Dutch mariners' accounts pirated the Amsterdam text, into which he added material from another source. Soon after, two further editors pirated this text for their own compilations. At the turn of the eighteenth century, one of the versions of Van den Broecke's text in these three compilations was translated into French and included in a collection of voyages made on behalf of the Dutch East India Company. Presumably, these editions were meant to celebrate Dutch enterprise in the East Indies and encourage investment in the Company.

The original manuscript attracted scholarly attention after it was purchased by the Dutch publishing house Martinus Nijhoff in November 1869 and was donated to the library of the University of Leiden. Through the early twentieth century, it was Dutch scholars who made use of the manuscript in their studies of the early imperial history of the Netherlands' East Indian empire. The manuscript's accessibility was greatly enhanced after Martinus Nijhoff published transcriptions of the manuscript's African and Indian sections in 1950 and 1962–3, respectively, on behalf of the Linschoten Society; K. Ratelband edited

[1] For a bibliographic listing of these and subsequent editions, see the appendix on 'Earlier Editions'.

the transcription of the African portions while W. P. Coolhaas edited the Indian parts. Ratelband's edition of the manuscript has since become the version most frequently used by Africanist scholars who can read Dutch. It is particularly useful for its biography of Van den Broecke and for its notes on the personalities of the Netherlands' commercial elite. Scholars interested in those subjects will still find the Ratelband edition rewarding. I have incorporated many, but not all, of these notes into the following edition. However, though Ratelband's edition was 'well done' on the Dutch side of Van den Broecke's experience, its African aspects were relatively 'raw' in the light of recent Africanist scholarship.[1] Hence, I have found much work to do, in addition to my effort to transform the text of Van den Broecke's manuscript from a haphazardly composed record handwritten in seventeenth-century Dutch into a deliberately and clearly organized printed document in modern English.

I have been fortunate to receive a great amount of help. I began this project in 1993 as my MA degree thesis, which required that I demonstrate analytical proficiency in the primary sources in my field of study, the pre-colonial history of West Africa.[2] Financial support came from a Dupont Fellowship from the Corcoran Department of History and the Graduate School of Arts and Sciences of the University of Virginia, which enabled me to travel to the Netherlands and study the modern Dutch language at the University of Leiden in the summer of 1993. Once I was back in Charlottesville and beginning to translate and annotate the text, several professors assisted me. I offer hearty thanks to Professors Larry Goedde, John Stagg, and my tireless advisor, Joe Miller. Adam Jones of the University of Leipzig gave a full reading of the thesis version, and provided an avalanche of helpful suggestions on how to go about improving every aspect of my work.

In 1996 I moved to Leiden and the Research School CNWS to begin dissertation research on a different but related topic, and used spare moments to

[1] This descriptive terminology was coined by Adam Jones, in his *Raw, Medium, Well Done: A Critical Review of Editorial and Quasi-Editorial Work on Pre–1885 European Sources for Sub-Saharan Africa*.

[2] I should add that at the time I was also under the influence of the essays in the special issue of the journal *Paideuma* (33, 1987) on the 'use and abuse' of European sources for African history, and in particular of the suggestion of Adam Jones that '*every* historian of Africa who works partly with written sources should in his or her own interests attempt to prepare at least one edition, however short'. Jones, 'A Critique of Editorial and Quasi-Editorial Work on pre-1885 European Sources for Sub-Saharan Africa, 1960–1986', with emphasis in the original.

expand the translation and notes, and finally bring this project to a conclusion. I thank Ilona Beumer and Willem Vogelsang for welcoming me as a guest at the CNWS; and the library staff at the Afrika Studiecentrum and at the University's *dousa* (special collections department); and also the conservators at Kenwood House and English Heritage; and further thanks to my friend Professor Robert Ross, to my editor, Professor Robin Law, and to my neighbour on the Kloksteeg, Ywan von Dewall, for their encouragement, assistance and good cheer.

Leiden, 21 February 2000

INTRODUCTION

Pieter van den Broecke traded on the fringes of Portugal's Atlantic commercial empire and of several separate regional economies in Africa in the very early seventeenth century. His manuscript primarily details the commercial organization of metropolitan Dutch merchant houses entering the African trade and the trading strategy of their agents, men like Van den Broecke himself, who were on the African coast. The manuscript also presents information about political, economic and cultural affairs specific to the time in the West African areas of Senegambia and the Gold Coast, and in the Central African regions of Loango and Sonyo.

Pieter van den Broecke was born at a pivotal time in western European economic history. He was born into a commercial family in Antwerp on 25 February 1585.[1] During the previous century, Antwerp merchants had established the city as the principal trade emporium of Europe. At Antwerp, merchants collected and distributed the staples of long-distance commerce. There were stockpiles of copper and iron from Germany, silks and luxury goods from Italy and the Levant, woollen cloth from England, and spices from the Portuguese colonial empire. Antwerp was also a manufacturing centre for two important high-value trade items, cloth and sugar. By 1550 there were nineteen sugar refineries in Antwerp applying heat and chemicals to partially refined 'brown' *muscovado* sugar from Portugal's Atlantic colonies to process it into the white, high-grade granular sweetener which was then finding a growing consumer base throughout Europe.[2] Both sides of Pieter van den Broecke's family were involved in Antwerp's booming sugar industry. On his mother's side, her father

[1] Extract of Van den Broecke family 'Memorie-boek', in Pieter van den Broecke's manuscript, f. 128v. The manuscript is conserved at the library of the University of Leiden, the Netherlands, and is catalogued there by the designation BPL 952. The extract is also reprinted in Ratelband, *Reizen naar West-Afrika van Pieter van den Broecke,* as appendix 3.

[2] Israel, *Dutch Primacy in World Trade*, pp.1–5; Braudel, *The Wheels of Commerce*, II, pp. 191–3.

Pieter and uncle Jasper de Morimont were sugar refiners, and there were generations of refiners on his father's side also.[1] By 1585, the year of Van den Broecke's birth, Antwerp's commerce was suffering as the city became a focus of conflict in the so-called Eighty Years War between Spain and the 'rebel' northern Dutch provinces. The Spanish laid siege to Antwerp in late 1584, recaptured the city a year later, and declared a total embargo on Dutch shipping. The States-General at The Hague retaliated by sending forces south to blockade the estuary of the River Scheldt, which was Antwerp's only access to the sea, thereby making sea-borne trade to and from the southern, 'Spanish' Netherlands risky, unpredictable and inconvenient. The Van den Broecke family joined a northward exodus of Antwerp's merchant and industrial elite fleeing in search of better places to do business.[2]

The Van den Broecke family settled first in the northern Netherlands town of Alkmaar on 17 August 1586, but left less than a year later for Hamburg.[3] Unlike Alkmaar, Hanseatic ports in north-western Germany such as Hamburg were officially neutral and therefore not subject to the Spanish embargo on shipping. Ships registered there could call safely at Iberian-controlled ports to load *muscovado* sugar for shipment to Hansa refineries. Alternatively, neutrally-flagged ships could obtain licenses from Lisbon to carry semi-finished sugar from merchant sellers in the colonies via the capital, where they paid taxes, and finally to northern Europe to be refined.[4] Transhipments of Brazilian *muscovado* via Lisbon to Hamburg turned the city into a haven for emigrant Flemish sugar refiners.

Through the 1590s a series of decisive Dutch military victories over the Spanish and the flood of over 100,000 working-class refugees from the Spanish Netherlands to the north favoured the emergence of the United Provinces as the new entrepôt for long-distance, high-value commodity trade. In 1590 the Spanish king Philip II withdrew most of his forces facing the Dutch and threw them into the civil war then unfolding in France. Dutch forces then recaptured critical river and overland trade routes to Germany and Italy in the south, and across the Ems estuary to Emden in the north. Philip also lifted the embargo on Dutch shipping with the Iberian peninsula, and Dutch navies squashed Flemish

[1] Ratelband, *Reizen naar West-Afrika*, pp. xxi–xxiv.

[2] Israel, *Dutch Primacy in World Trade*, pp. 30, 34; Brulez, 'De Diaspora der Vlaamse kooplui op het einde der XVIe eeuw'.

[3] Ratelband, *Reizen naar West-Afrika*, p. xxii.

[4] See, for example, the Lübeck ship in Van den Broecke's journal entry for 27 June 1606.

privateering sufficiently to achieve significantly lower insurance and shipping costs in Dutch bottoms.[1] Working-class immigrants provided an infusion of cheap skilled labour to the cloth-manufacturing towns of Haarlem and Leiden in the northern Netherlands, stimulating investment in textile production and distribution.[2] Amsterdam attracted exiles from Antwerp like the Van den Broecke family, who returned there from Hamburg around 1597,[3] and their sugar-refining in-laws, the De Morimont brothers.[4] It also attracted Portuguese Sephardi Jewish and 'New Christian' merchants, who controlled supplies of Brazilian *muscovado*. In 1595 the States-General extended their blockade of the Scheldt to the entire Spanish Netherlands coast, including such Flemish ports as Dunkirk, which the Sephardi used to distribute the semi-finished sugar to refiners in north-west Germany. After 1595 Sephardi merchants had to move to new distribution sites, principally Amsterdam, where they could receive *muscovado* sugar trans-shipped through neutral countries or carried directly from Brazil under false papers.[5] Most Amsterdam refiners bypassed Lisbon contractors and used the contacts they had developed while in Antwerp with 'enemy' Portuguese planters on the Atlantic islands of the Canaries, Madeira and São Tomé to send Dutch ships there directly to load *muscovado*.[6] Dutch bottoms carried perhaps as much as two-thirds of Brazilian sugar prior to1600.[7]

This community of elite immigrant merchants also collaborated to finance high-risk capital-intensive trade missions throughout the furthest reaches of the Iberian empire, including the Americas, the East Indies and Western Africa. Single voyages were financed by a shipping firm, the Dutch *partenrederij* (lit. 'shared outfitting'), which spread the cost of renting bottoms, hiring crews, supplying cargo, and arranging insurance among several investors, who were usually general merchants with interests in many other branches of the Netherlands' far-reaching commercial enterprise. Upon safe return of the ship,

[1] Israel, *Dutch Primacy in World Trade*, pp. 30, 38–42.

[2] Boxer, *The Dutch Seaborne Empire*, pp. 20–21.

[3] Ratelband, *Reizen naar West-Afrika*, p. xxvi.

[4] Pieter and Jasper de Morimont tried but failed to establish their refinery in Leiden, but succeeded in Amsterdam; on the brothers, see Reesse, *De suikerhandel van Amsterdam*, p. 105.

[5] Israel, 'The Economic Contribution of the Dutch Sephardhi Jewry to Holland's Golden Age'.

[6] Ratelband, *Reizen naar West-Afrika*, pp. xxv, xxix.

[7] Cited in Schwartz, *Sugar Plantations in the Formation of Brazilian Society*, p. 161.

its cargo was auctioned off; after the debts incurred had been met, the investors (*reders*) split the profits, if there were any.[1] A shipwreck or insufficient return cargo brought spectacular losses. More affluent metropolitan merchants insulated themselves from such short-term boom-or-bust returns by organizing joint-stock 'companies' to support repeated trade operations. The Dutch firms entering the African trade were probably organized in the same manner as the so-called *vóórcompagnieën* (lit. 'pre-companies') trading in the East Indies before the formation of the Dutch East India Company in 1602. A few wealthy merchants provided the initial capital to open and register the firm and then attracted less affluent subscribers (*participenten*) to buy smaller fractions of the shares which they owned. These *participenten* had no input into the operation of the company; they hoped to reap annual dividends and perhaps sell their shares for more than they paid for them. The richer merchants retained control of the company and served as its directors (*bewindhebbers*), devising strategy, choosing destinations, appropriate cargoes and suitable agents according to the latest reports and rumours about trade conditions in faraway places.[2]

Dutch commerce in Africa expanded explosively in the very early seventeenth century, with some 200 ships sailing there in the decade 1599–1608.[3] Most of these early Dutch merchants obtained African products from neglected Portuguese colonial outposts, such as hides from Arguim, an island off the coast of modern Mauretania, and a little gold from São Jorge da Mina ('St George of the Mine', later called Elmina), on the appropriately named Gold Coast (modern Ghana).[4] These traders were too weak to seize by force these old coastal depots, which the Portuguese still guarded with imperial

[1] Boxer, *The Dutch Seaborne Empire*, pp. 8, 18–9; Postma, *The Dutch in the Atlantic Slave Trade*, pp. 9, 17–8.

[2] Unfortunately the history of Guinea *vóórcompagnineën* has not yet been explored in any detail comparable to those trading in the East. The description above is a conflation of the literature on Dutch companies trading in the East Indies prior to the VOC and reports on commercial strategies and organization included in Pieter van den Broecke's manuscript. For the literature on the *vóórcompagnineën*, see Steensgaard, 'The Companies as a Specific Institution in the History of European Expansion'.

[3] Unger, 'Nieuwe gegevens betreffende het begin der vaart op Guinea', p. 208.

[4] The Portuguese established their station at Arguim, a small island 6 km off Cap Blanc, in 1448. Portuguese merchants there traded for (in addition to hides) a little gold dust, slaves, ostrich feathers, gum and salt; see Brooks, *Landlords and Strangers*, pp. 125–7. The Portuguese established their fort at Elmina on the Gold Coast in 1482: for its foundation and early history, see Hair, *The Founding of the Castelo São Jorge da Mina*.

troops and cannon, nor could they conquer inland sources controlled by African aristocrats.[1] Thus Dutch merchants were unable to capture older, established connections to African regional economies, which had good supplies of high-value commodities such as slaves, top-grade ivory and, especially, gold. Therefore Dutch merchants like Van den Broecke developed, on behalf of their firms, new points of access to these same regional markets. They offered superior-quality textiles at better rates as immediate payment for as much gold as they could find, but mostly for lower-value African exports, such as ivory, hides, dye-wood and palm-cloths. Thus they invested in developing personal contacts with African aristocrats who controlled new trade ports and in luring other established local traders, including both African elites and Portuguese contractors, away from their old obligations.

Van den Broecke's manuscript describes very complex commercial strategies of Dutch merchants of this generation, who organized co-operation between their private firms to fix prices on the coast, open new ports, post temporarily resident factors to work with local African political authorities, bulk export cargoes, and relay messages and orders from *bewindhebbers* to their agents on the African coast. Pro-war anti-Spanish political factions in the United Provinces periodically pushed for the amalgamation of the smaller companies into a single parastatal monopoly company, which would be armed to overrun Portuguese strongpoints on the African coast.[2] Provincially-minded merchants in Zeeland and young upstarts in Amsterdam, however, were cool to the idea of subordinating their reasonably prosperous trade to a cartel of older and ambitious Amsterdam elites, who were themselves resistant to diminishing their personal control in a new amalgamated company structure.[3] When several Amsterdam companies did come together in 1599 as the *Vereenigde Compagnie* ('United Company', which was later renamed the Guinea Company)[4] it was probably nothing more than a veneer of metropolitan unity among *bewindhebbers* which barely concealed continuing intense competition

[1] A more developed discussion of the military inferiority of European merchants to powerful African elites is central to the thesis of Thornton, *Africa and the Africans in the Making of the Atlantic World*, pp. 36–40, 112–16.

[2] This is precisely what was accomplished with the chartering of the West India Company in 1621, after the Twelve Years' Truce with Spain ended.

[3] Unger, 'Nieuwe gegevens', p. 208; Israel, *Dutch Primacy in World Trade*, p. 61.

[4] Postma, *The Dutch in the Atlantic Slave Trade*, p. 17.

among their agents on the African coast. The most effective means of eliminating intra-Dutch competition was always *ad hoc* collusion on the coast itself among merchants, like Van den Broecke, at individual African ports.

Van den Broecke's manuscript is composed as an occasional register of five trips as a merchant or factor, covering four trade missions to Africa and one to the Indies. His voyages took him successively further south and, eventually, far to the east. He gradually rose in rank from an employee at an Amsterdam merchant house to junior factor (*ondercommies*) on his first and second African voyages, to senior factor (*oppercommies*) on his third and fourth trips, to tough-fighting senior merchant (*opperkoopman*) in the East Indies.

Though Van den Broecke did not always disclose which merchant firms he represented along the way, parts of his career are known. In 1602, the seventeen-year-old Van den Broecke began his employment, probably as a sort of apprentice, at the Amsterdam merchant house of Bartholomus Moor and Marten Hooftman.[1] Three years later he left this position in Amsterdam for a job as junior factor on an Africa-bound ship and a handsome salary of twenty guilders per month. His new employer was almost certainly Elias Trip, a diversified merchant-industrialist who climbed to the highest reaches of the Amsterdam elite during the first decade of the seventeenth century.[2] Elias and his brother Jacob were originally from Dordrecht, where they were arms-dealers who used the river traffic from Liège in cannons and munitions to satisfy the States-General's demand for weapons. Trip also owned several ships and a salt works in Dordrecht, and was an importer of Swedish copper and German iron.[3]

This venture took Van den Broecke from Dordrecht to the Cape Verde coast (modern Senegal) to trade iron bars against African hides, ambergris, rice, wax, and small amounts of ivory and gold. Van den Broecke did very little trading of his own on this trip; most of the trade was supervised by the chief factor. Van den Broecke spent six months ashore at Portudal on the Petite Côte (the 'Little Coast', as Europeans named the area just south of Cape Verde) and another month coasting offshore. This first voyage's relatively simple strategy of trading at the edge of the Sahara desert was punctuated by a battle against a

[1] See Van den Broecke's journal entry for 16 November1605; Ratelband, *Reizen naar West-Afrika*, p. xxx.

[2] Van den Broecke made no mention of Trip in his manuscript, but the published editions did: Van den Broecke, *Korte Historiael* (Haarlem edition), ff. 2v, 5r.

[3] Klein, *De Trippen in de 17e Eeuw*.

Lisbon-bound ship off Joal, a town on the Senegalese coast. The Lisbon-bound ship was captured and its cargo of São Tomé sugar, a few elephant tusks and bales of cotton, and ninety very weakened slaves was seized. The Portuguese crew was put ashore and the slaves were quickly sold off to an English ship for victuals and water for the voyage home.

A year after his return from that trip, Van den Broecke left again for Africa, this time on behalf of a consortium of Amsterdam merchants who would also sponsor his subsequent trips to western central Africa. The composition of this company is difficult to discern, as it changed over time as controlling shares were bought and sold. Jacques (or, in the Dutch form of the name, Jacob) Niquet was certainly one of the company's directors.[1] Niquet was of the same small circle of wealthy Antwerp émigré merchant families in Amsterdam as Van den Broecke, in which family and business relationships were closely interwoven. Niquet's sister Maria was married to Bartholomes Moor, Van den Broecke's first employer. Niquet's other sister Margaretha was married to Gerard (or Gerrit) Reynst, an Amsterdam merchant who may have been another of the company's directors. Reynst had been centrally involved in the formation of the *Vereenigde Oostindische Compagnie* (United East India Company, known by the Dutch acronym VOC) in 1602. He also played a pioneering role in establishing Dutch trade with western central Africa; his firm, 'Gerrit Reynst and Company' was named by the States-General on 6 August 1610 as the first Dutch company to have traded in 'Angola'.[2] The Amsterdam merchant Frans Jacobsz Hinloopen was also involved in directing the company, at least by 28 January 1613, when an Amsterdam notary produced a letter of credentials for Van den Broecke. The letter explained that Van den Broecke had made 'several trips' on behalf of the company of Hinloopen, Niquet, and two other Amsterdam merchant-investors, Pieter Jansz Reael and Jacob Dirksz de Lange, in whose employ he then still honourably stood.[3] The Antwerp-born Amsterdam merchant Samuel Bloomaert may also have been involved with the

[1] Van den Broecke did not name Jacques Niquet as his sponsor in his manuscript, but this was indicated in the introduction to the published editions; Van den Broecke, *Korte Historiael* (Haarlem edition), f. 2v. For Niquet, see also Elias, *De Vroedschap van Amsterdam*, I, pp. 307–8.

[2] Van Deursen, *Resolutiën der Staten-Generaal, Part I, 1610–1612*, pp. 189,196. Reynst was named Governor-General in 1613 by the VOC and travelled with Van den Broecke on the latter's first voyage to the East Indies. He died on 7 December 1615 at Jakarta: Elias, *Vroedschap*, I, p. 373.

[3] Amsterdam Gemeente Archief, Notariael Archief, J. Bruyningh, 28 January 1613. Hinloopen and Reael were married to sisters: Elias, *Vroedschap*, I, pp. 260–61, 311.

company at some point. Bloomaert was a veteran of three VOC voyages between 1603 and 1609. After returning to Amsterdam, he became an investor in African trade, often co-operating with Hinloopen. On 5 June 1612, he married Reynst's daughter, Catherina. Upon the formation of the *Westindische Compagnie* (West India Company, WIC) in 1621, he became one its directors, and after his death in 1651 his papers helped inform Olfert Dapper's massive geography, published in 1668.[1] The company of Bloomaert, Hinloopen, and two other Amsterdam merchants, was named in 1624 (but presumably referring to trading in earlier years, before the formation of the WIC) as sponsors of Joost Gerritsz Lijnbaen,[2] who appears to have been working for the same company as Van den Broecke in1612.[3]

Van den Broecke's first voyage on behalf of this Amsterdam company took him far to the south of Cape Verde, to the Grain Coast,[4] the Gold Coast, the area of western central Africa north of the river Congo called Loango, and the Sonyo province of north-western Kongo which lay just south of the river. This was the effective limit of Dutch shipping at the time, since the coast to the south was controlled by the Portuguese in Angola. Unlike on the first voyage to Cape Verde, Van den Broecke personally traded often, bargaining Dutch textiles against West African gold and West-Central African ivory. While the Netherlands was at war with the Iberian monarchy, Dutch ships could not obtain gold from the Portuguese forts on the Gold Coast under its control, the most important of which was the castle at Elmina. On Van den Broecke's trip to the Gold Coast, he encountered several Dutch ships trading with merchants of the African kingdom of Asebu just west of Elmina at the fishing village of

[1] On Blommaert, see Jones, 'Decompiling Dapper', pp. 179–84. See also Van den Broecke's journal entry for 22 April 1612, and annotation thereto.

[2] Van Wassenaer, *Historisch verhael* (October 1624), f. 28r. The company was referred to as 'Hinlopen, Blommert, Steenhuyssen, and Lucas van der Venne'. Lucas van der Venne appears to have also run a company at times in competition with Van den Broecke's outfit; see Van den Broecke's journal entries for 16 March 1610 and 19 March 1610. On 12 October 1613, Van der Venne attested a notarized letter for Samuel Brun, after his first trip Africa as a surgeon for a Dutch company. This letter is reprinted in Naber, *Samuel Brun's Schiffarten*, p. 97. An annotated English translation of Brun's account is included in Jones, *German Sources for West African History*, pp. 44–96.

[3] See Van den Broecke's journal entry for 22 April 1612.

[4] This section of the coast, corresponding to what is nowadays Liberia, was named in early times for the so-called 'Grains of Paradise', known now as malaguetta, which Europeans purchased there. These 'grains' were the peppery-tasting dried fruits of the plant *Aframonum melegueta*, which was indigenous to this region. See Van den Broecke's journal entry for 25 February 1608.

Mouri. His manuscript indicates intense private activity there prior to the States-General's decision to establish a government post, Fort Nassau, at Mouri in 1611. In western central Africa, Van den Broecke again worked the periphery of the area under Portuguese influence, traded for ivory in Loango and visited Sonyo, an increasingly separatist province of the Kongo kingdom, which was itself allied with the Portuguese in Angola. His manuscript is suggestively silent on his economic activity there, though it describes the politics and customs of the court in detail. This part of the manuscript is composed in a slightly different manner, including long and somewhat uninspired descriptions of African flora and fauna; these may have been a deliberate attempt to re-work a rough set of original notes and commercial records of prices and accounting which he had made for his employers into a travelogue of more general interest for future publication.

Van den Broecke left for his third voyage to Africa a month before the Twelve Years' Dutch-Iberian truce was signed in October 1609. Elmina-bound Portuguese caravels carried that news past Van den Broecke while he was anchored off Portudal on the Senegalese coast. On this voyage, Van den Broecke, now chief factor, travelled directly to western central Africa to sell textiles for ivory, African cloth and *takula*, a red dyewood. His manuscript describes Dutch and Portuguese merchants transporting foreign and imported cloth, takula and ivory within the region; for Dutch merchants like Van den Broecke, the trading strategy was to carry goods within the regional economy to areas of demand and scarcity, and eventually convert the series of local exchanges into the form of high-value ivory for the Amsterdam market. The manuscript is thus very specific on the character and values of, and demand for, different types of European and African cloth.

Van den Broecke's fourth trip to Africa came in 1611 and took the same course of navigation and trade as his previous voyage. He added to this part of his manuscript a lengthy report on the kingdom of Loango, the place where he had spent most of his time in Africa and where he had become a friend and trading partner of the *mani* (or, 'king'[1] of) Loango. His report is largely a synthesis of the geographic and trade notes from his descriptions of his three previous trips there, but it is also supplemented with new observations about the food, dress, customs, religion and politics of the people of Loango.

Van den Broecke was subsequently hired by the mighty VOC as a chief factor in 1613. He probably obtained this posting through the benefactors of his

[1] In West-Central Africa, the title *mani* (often abbreviated to *ma*) denoted a person of authority. Van den Broecke made it clear in his manuscript that the *mani* Loango was the

African voyages, many of whom were also heavy investors in the VOC. His first voyage to the Indies was very eventful. He left in July 1613 accompanying an India-bound fleet as far as Madagascar, then sailed a yacht north to Arabia. There he established the first Dutch factory at Aden in 1614 and travelled inland to the Yemeni capital Sana'a.[1] In 1616 he was sent by the Governor-General of the Indies, Jan Pietersz Coen, to establish another factory at Surat and to direct VOC trade in Hindustan.[2] He later led the defence of the fort of Jakarta (or Jacatra, as it was known at the time) against the British, who were allied with the Javanese. He was shipwrecked and was held prisoner by the Javanese for over four months. Upon his escape he returned to Surat, where he served until 1629. During this first tour of the East, Van den Broecke fathered at least three children: the first was a daughter born to a free Turkish woman at Mokka, named Issa Ibben Soliman, but this child died at just ten years of age, in mid-1628.[3] An Indian slave at Surat, named Gaddom Garri (baptized Maria), bore him a son Pieter on 1 May 1628;[4] another Indian slave, Logia, bore him a second son Johan (Jan) on 20 February 1629:[5] both of these sons were recorded to be VOC soldiers as of 1 August 1640. Another putative son, Paulus van den Broeke, was awarded a VOC land grant (*perken*) in 1628 to run a nutmeg plantation on the Moluccan island of Pulu Ay.[6] In 1630 Van den Broecke took command of a homeward-bound fleet of Indiamen which carried, in addition to Asian riches, the widow of Governor-General Coen.[7] Upon his return to Amsterdam on 8 June 1630,[8] the VOC awarded him a gold chain worth 1,200 guilders.[9]

'king' of this region. He also recorded other persons of lesser authority who bore other *mani* titles; see for example his journal entry for 31 January 1610.

[1] Synopses of Van den Broecke's activities in Yemen and Sana'a are available: Brouwer, 'Le Voyage au Yémen de Pieter van den Broecke'; Brouwer, 'Under the Watchful Eye of Mimī Bin ʿAbd Allāh: The Voyage of the Dutch Merchant Pieter van den Broecke to the Court of Djaʿfar Bāshā in Sana'a'.

[2] For translated excerpts of his experience at Surat, see Moreland, 'Pieter van den Broecke at Surat, 1620–29'. See also the translation: Narain and Sharma, *A Contemporary Dutch Chronicle of Mughal India*.

[3] Van den Broecke family 'Memorie-Boek' extract, f. 129v. Van den Broecke recorded that he had received news on 10 October 1628 about the girl's death five months before.

[4] Ibid., f. 129v.

[5] Ibid., f. 129v.

[6] Rick van den Broeke, personal communication, 11 April 1998; Van de Wall, *Nederlandsche Oudheden in de Molukken*, p. 288.

[7] Ratelband, *Reizen naar West-Afrika*, pp. xxxv–xliv; Coolhaas, *Pieter van den Broecke in Azië*.

[8] Van den Broecke, *Korte Historiael* (Haarlem edition), f. 144r. The month was there misprinted as 'Julij' (July), but should be June; Coolhaas, *Van den Broecke in Azië*, II, p. 370 n.8.

[9] Van den Broecke, *Korte Historiael* (Haarlem edition), f. 144r.

Between his arrival in Amsterdam and his second and last departure for the Indies, he worked on the manuscript under consideration here, and sat for a portrait by his friend Frans Hals.[1] The purpose of the portrait and publication of the manuscript are clearly related. The portrait was probably completed in 1633; that same year, a mutual friend of Van den Broecke and Hals, Adriaen Jacobz Matham, reproduced the painted portrait as an engraving, which was then used as frontispiece of the version of Van den Broecke's journal which was published in 1634.[2] The portrait (and the engraving from it) deliberately showed Van den Broecke as something greater than an ordinary trader. The gold chain awarded to him by the VOC is immediately noticeable, as is his hand, which rests on a cane, a prop usually employed to indicate political authority.[3] The engraver added a quatrain to celebrate his patriotic achievements:

> This is the Van den Broecke, who astounded the Persians
> When the Batavian first came roaring across the Red Sea,
> Who, on the continents of Arabia and Indus,
> First fostered trade for the Dutch nation.[4]

Van den Broecke probably wrote the manuscript under consideration here and commissioned the portrait and engraving to lobby the VOC directors for a new contract and, perhaps, a promotion to the VOC's controlling *Raad van Indië* ('Indian Council'). After the book was published, he was offered a new contract as senior merchant (*opperkoopman*) on 25 August 1634, and soon left for the East Indies again. He died six years later on 1 December 1640, succumbing to sudden illness during the Dutch conquest of the Portuguese station at Malacca.[5]

[1] A copy of this portrait appears as the frontispiece to this book.

[2] Van den Broecke is listed as the first witness and Matham as the second witness to the baptism of Hals's daughter Susana in 1634; see Grimm, *Frans Hals*. For the dating of the portrait see Van Gelder, 'Dateering van Frans Hals' portret van P. v. d. Broecke'.

[3] Larry Goedde, personal communication, 5 August 1994.

[4] 'Dit is die van den Broeck, die Parssen deed' verwondren/ Doen eerst den Batavier op 't Roode meijr quam donderen./Die bij den Arabier en Indus was te land./ Die eerst voot 't Hollants volck den handel heeft geplant.' Van den Broecke was something of an amateur poet and may have written these lines himself. The back pages of the manuscript contain two poems written in his hand, one in Spanish and the other in French. The Dutch text is somewhat awkward and the resulting literal English translation somewhat stilted. A more free and rhyming literary translation (more appropriate to the genre) would be: 'This is yon Van den Broeck, who made the Persians wonder;/ While his Batavian guns shook the Red Sea with thunder/ Set foot on the Arabian's and Indus land/ The tree of Holland's trade an acorn in his hand.' Ywan von Dewall set this into rhyme and metre; personal communication, 7 April 1998.

[5] Coolhaas, *Van den Broecke in Azië*, II, p. 396 n.1.

Although the manuscript is structured as a daily log, it is not a contemporaneously kept diary. It has a final date of 30 October 1612 affixed to its African parts, but Van den Broecke certainly did not write those portions of his manuscript concerning his African voyages until later—probably eighteen years later, at least, after he returned to Amsterdam from the East Indies. The last date Van den Broecke affixed to the manuscript is 1 January 1630, when his manuscript abruptly ends with his homeward-bound fleet about to leave the town of Bantam, on the northern coast of the island of Java. The manuscript shows signs that Van den Broecke re-worked earlier rough notes of his experiences in Africa after he returned from the Indies in 1630. For example, he repeatedly used Arabic and Malay words to describe things he saw in Africa—*prau* for Gold Coast canoes, *pagger* for the fence around the *mani* Loango's compound; and he described African kola as 'like the Indian *siri pinnan*'. On one occasion, he wrote 'Jaccara' (for Jacatra, i.e. Jakarta) before correcting himself with 'Accra'. Such Asian words could only have been used after he travelled to the East Indies. These same words are also evidence that Van den Broecke personally authored the manuscript in its present form, since a ghost-writer or editor would not have used such terms.

The African portions of Van den Broecke's manuscript were composed independently of the existing description of the coast most similar to it, Samuel Brun's *Schiffarten*.[1] The two texts present similar information,[2] but without any glaring plagiarism. What aspects they do share can be attributed to the two author's similar northern European backgrounds and the near contemporaneity of their trips to the same parts of western central Africa.[3] Also, they traveled within the same circle of Dutch mariners and merchants, and so it is possible that at least some of the similarities in their texts could be attributed to shared mariner lore about the places they visited, which they recorded as personal experiences. Van den Broecke left the Loango coast on his last trip to Africa in June 1612; Samuel Brun left Europe in December 1611 for his first

[1] Originally published in Basel in 1624 with the title *Samuel Brun, des Wundartzt und Burgers zu Basel, Schiffarten* ..., and published in a modern edition in 1913 by the Linschoten Society, edited by S. P. l'Honoré Naber. An annotated English translation is included in Jones, *German Sources*, pp. 44–96.

[2] A systematic comparison of these similarities appears in the notes to Adam Jones' translation of Brun: in Jones, *German Sources*, pp. 44–96.

[3] This conclusion that the two works, though similar, are independent also has support from Jones, 'Double Dutch: A Survey of Seventeenth-Century German Sources for West African History', p. 142.

trip to Loango,[1] probably arriving the summer that Van den Broecke left. The earliest that Van den Broecke could have had read Brun's book would have been when he returned from the Indies in 1630; Brun's book was first published in German in 1624 and republished three times in German and once in Latin during the following three years.[2] Given the general similarities between Dutch and German, Van den Broecke (or his family residing in Hamburg) should have been able to make sense of Brun's text, but there is no clear evidence that Van den Broecke ever consulted Brun's published work.

Van den Broecke's manuscript also opens a window for historians to peer into the world of producing and publishing travellers' journals in early modern times. The survival of Van den Broecke's handwritten draft for his published version is very unusual among early descriptions of Africa,[3] and is unique among the remarkable corpus of seventeenth-century Dutch texts concerning Africa. Authors and printers routinely discarded their handwritten texts after they had been set into print. Where authors' manuscript drafts survive for books outside of African history, they provide a rich ground for intellectual inquiry for bibliographers and literary critics. A dozen or more academic journals are devoted to this very subject. For scholars interested in pre-colonial African history, the Van den Broecke manuscript thus presents a valuable opportunity to explore similar issues relating to authorship, seventeenth-century publishing, and the production of historical information.

Three sorts of concerns for historians are noted here – in addition to the rigour normally required in the study of early published primary texts. The greatest difference between the manuscript and the published editions is that approximately two-thirds of the content of Van den Broecke's manuscript was omitted in the published edition. Van den Broecke himself may have wished some of his material never to appear in print. His disparaging comments about prominent colleagues might have been professionally unwise while he was

[1] Van den Broecke was acquainted with the master of Brun's ship, Jan Pieterssen. They met off the coast of Loango to arrange a price-fixing agreement; see journal entries for 16 March 1610 and 19 March 1610.

[2] Jones, *German Sources*, p. 44.

[3] See the excellent variorum edition of Jean Barbot's English edition of 1732 and his French manuscript of 1688; Hair, Jones, and Law, *Barbot on Guinea*, published by the Hakluyt Society in 1992. A handful of early Portuguese manuscripts saw contemporaneous publishing under their authors' names; see Fage, *Original Sources for Precolonial Western Africa Published in European Languages*). On the relationship between Friar Cavazzi's manuscript and his printed text, see Thornton, 'New Light on Cavazzi's Seventeenth-Century Description of Kongo'.

seeking promotion in the VOC,[1] and the release of sensitive commercial intelligence and nautical information which he had recorded might have upset his benefactors.

The published texts also added a few small items of information not seen in the manuscript, and these present a conundrum for historians concerned with 'primary' sources. Here I follow David Henige's definition of primary sources as 'those pieces of information which stand in the most intimate relationship to an event or process *in the present state of our knowledge*'.[2] Taken as a whole, Van den Broecke's manuscript would bear the closest relationship to his experiences in Africa, even though, as indicated above, I believe the manuscript to be a later (circa 1630) compilation of notes, now lost, which he made while there in 1605–12. However, historically significant pieces of information scattered throughout the printed text which are not seen in the manuscript may also qualify as 'primary sources', if one can establish that Van den Broecke was indeed their source.

The Haarlem edition introduced the text with two poems celebrating the author's heroics, the engraved frontispiece, and an elaborate dedication of the book from the author to the 'honourable directors' of the VOC.[3] Van den Broecke's dedication is of interest because it identifies Jacques Niquet as having sponsored his journeys to 'Angola'.[4] In the body of the text, the printed edition also made unique claims about Van den Broecke's personal commercial achievements. Take, for example, the printed text's assertion that Van den Broecke had established the first Dutch factory at Loango:

> den 8 Februarij, hebbe ick de eerste van de Nederlantsche natie aen 't Landt, (niet teghenstaende een onghesonde plaetse is) een Comptoir ghestabileert, daer te vooren niemant, als 't scheep, heeft durven handelen, 't welck ick verstae tsedert dien tijdt, altijt, geobserveert te zijn.[5]

On the 8th of February [1610] I established the first Dutch office onshore

[1] His criticism of Wemmer van Barcham in his journal entries for 22 April 1608 and 23 April 1608 was omitted, for example.

[2] Henige, 'The Race is Not Always to the Swift: Thoughts on the Use of Written Sources for the Study of Early African History', p. 54; emphasis in the original.

[3] The first celebratory poem was unsigned, and was perhaps written by Van den Broecke himself. The second poem was signed simply 'C.V.K.' (perhaps referring to C. van Kittenstein of Haarlem).

[4] Van den Broecke, *Korte Historiael* (Haarlem edition), f. 2v.

[5] Ibid., f. 17r.

> (notwithstanding that it is an unhealthy place), as before this no one had dared to trade except aboard ship; I understand that since then it has been kept up.

The published texts similarly announced that Van den Broecke had opened an office at Mayoumba, in February 1612, to procure there dye-wood known as takula.[1] The authorship of the added material, although published under Van den Broecke's name, is impossible to identify positively. Nor is this added information necessarily historically accurate. The claim of having opened these 'offices' (the published text uses the French word *comptoir*, akin to the Dutch *kantoor*), for example, is dubious; Van den Broecke never mentioned in his manuscript anything other than temporary lodging arrangements.

Third, most of that third of the manuscript's contents which did get published was altered, by omitting some aspects, adding others, and in general giving new meanings to the manuscript's descriptions. When comparing the manuscript and printed texts, the most immediately striking difference lies in the changed spelling and grammar in the published editions. These alterations may be attributed to whoever set the type, as perhaps they did so according to their personal and dialectical conventions. These changes would thus reflect a re-working of Van den Broecke's Flemish style into the linguistic manners of northern Holland, and in particular Haarlem. There is also a small but noticeable and consistent re-working of the spellings and phrases of the Haarlem text in the Amsterdam edition, reflecting another layer of adaptation. Most of the toponyms and personal names which made it into the Haarlem edition were changed in spelling, thus making any historical argument based on the close scrutiny of proper names in that text more problematic.

Additionally, many items were rearranged within the text; typically this involved moving items from the summary reports about Cape Verde ('Manners and Life of the Blacks of Cape Verde') and Loango ('Description of the Kingdom of Loango') to daily entries. For example, Van den Broecke's description of the *mani* Loango's prescience included in his manuscript's report on Loango was moved to a daily entry in the printed text and a local name for Van den Broecke was added:

> NOTA: Dat den koninck eenighe daghen te vooren, den koopman Adam Vermeulen (van my daer ghelaten) gheroepen hadde, en hem geseght, letter op, op

[1] Ibid., f. 22r.

sulcken dagh sal den Fitor Macaße (alsoo my daer hieten) hier zijn, en dierghelijcke dinghen voor my mede brenghen, dat in der waerheydt, soo geschiede, als by velen daerby waren, notoir is gheweest.[1]

Note that several days before, the king had summoned the merchant Adam Vermuelen (whom I had left there), and told him: listen up, on such and such day shall the Fitor[2] Macasse (as I am called there) be here, and bring such things for me, which was true and did happen, as was noticed by many who were there.

Perhaps some of Van den Broecke's original descriptions were altered to polish his image in the eyes of his morally conservative metropolitan benefactors. For example, the manuscript's suggestive account of his encounter with *mani* Loango's sister, *mani* Lombo, reads as follows:

Ultijmo do. onboodt mij de connuckxsuster, genampt Manni Lombo, om bij haer to slappen; schonck mij een olifantstandt van 90 lb met een deel kruydt van bannanus, limmonnen, annanasus, boontiens ende diergelijcke vruchten meer. Sondt mij ontrent 18 man met een Portogisse amack om mij in te draghen ende te accompanieren tot in haer stadt die ontrent 1/2 dach rijssens te landewardts inlach.[3]

On the last day [of November 1610] the king's sister, named Manni Lombo, invited me to sleep with her. She gave me an elephant's tusk of 90 lb with vegetables like *bananas* [= plantains], limes, pineapples, beans, and other such fruits. Sent me around eighteen men with a Portuguese hammock to carry me and accompany me to her court, which lies about a half day's travel inland.

The manuscript is then suggestively silent for a month and half. In contrast, the Haarlem edition reads:

In de zelven maent noodichde my de Koninginne, ghenaemt Manny Lombe, op een jonghen Olifant te gast, om by haer my te slapen, liet my op haer Hoff, (ontrent 10 mijlen te landewaedt in) van haer dienaers halen, die my in een Amack (daer in lagh) tot daer toe droeghen: daer kommende, dede my met gheweld van den Olifant (dieder expresselijck om hadde laten doden) eten, die soo vreeselijck stonck, datter qualijck van wiert, ende sondt my daer naer weder nae huys, qualijck te vreden zijnde, met haer niet ten dienste wilden staen.[4]

1 Ibid., f. 17r, entry for 25 February 1612.
2 Portuguese *feitor*, 'factor, business agent'.
3 Van den Broecke manuscript, f. 12r, entry for 30 November 1610.
4 Van den Broecke, *Korte Historiael* (Haarlem edition), f. 19r.

> That same month [of November 1610], the queen, named Manny Lombe, invited me to visit her atop a young elephant [and] to sleep with her, at her court (which lay about ten miles inland). Had me fetched by her servants, who carried me there in a hammock (in which I lay). On arrival there, [she] forced me to eat of the elephant (which had been killed for that purpose), which stank so terribly that it made me sick, and sent me home again most upset that I would not service her.

This example, with its salacious elements, combines all of the muddling aspects of change. Van den Broecke's Dutch in the manuscript is considerably different from that of the printed text. The printed version removed some of manuscript's contents (the gifts), added others (the elephant), and changed much of what remained (the *mani*'s name, and the resolution of the titillating moral ambiguity previously left open to interpretation).

Van den Broecke's manuscript thus offers both challenge and reward. Reading it recalls the difficulty of sifting out credible detail from existing early documentation about Western Africa. The manuscript is a promising source for various economic and socio-political affairs on Africa's Atlantic coastline, as well as for the organization and strategy of early Dutch trade with the continent. But the opposite side of this coin is the ambiguity of this material (very powerfully impressed upon this editor in the process of translating the text) and the difficulty of discerning the situation surrounding the production of this and other early Dutch texts and, by extension, other early European language sources.

THE PRESENT EDITION

General

The text of this edition is an edited, annotated translation of four 'letters' from Pieter van den Broecke's manuscript. These four letters, which describe Van den Broecke's travels to Cape Verde, Guinea and Angola (16 November 1605–14 October 1606; 26 November 1607–4 June 1609; 17 August 1609–27 July 1611; 30 October 1611–16 September 1612) find their place in the manuscript before a subsequent letter describing Van den Broecke's voyage to the East Indies[1] (2 July 1613–1 January 1630). The final voyage to the East Indies did make a brief, uneventful stop to procure refreshments at Cape Lopez and Annobón, but those parts are not offered in translation here. Note also that the manuscript ends not with his return to the Netherlands from this voyage to the East Indies (as the published editions indeed do), but rather on 1 January 1630, when Van den Broecke was at Bantam on the island of Java, and just preparing to return home.

The original manuscript is conserved at the library of the University of Leiden, and is catalogued there by the designation BPL 952. I have worked with the original document, from a microfilm purchased from the library, and with Ratelband's 1950 edition of the text.

Presentation of the text

In transcribing the manuscript, I have tried to approximate the manuscript's structure and physical appearance as accurately as possible, and in particular have included Van den Broecke's side-notes to the text. Although some earlier editors have omitted such side-notes, I find that these glosses speak to two important aspects of the manuscript. First, the inclusion of these side-notes shows that Van den Broecke wrote this journal with the intention of getting it published, rather than just as a personal diary for his own reference. Secondly,

[1] An annotated transcription of Van den Broecke's entire travel account of the East Indies is also in print: Coolhaas, *Pieter van den Broecke in Azië*.

they show those areas towards which Van den Broecke himself wished to call readers' attention (scene changes, travails at sea, and his own heroics).

The manuscript also contains blank spaces where illustrations were apparently to be inserted after a description of some African exotica (e.g. 'An illustration of a chameleon in Loango'). While the versions published in 1634 inserted illustrations into such spaces, the present edition does not reproduce these images. I regard such illustrations as of spurious historical significance. Van den Broecke did not draw them; whoever did (they are unsigned) probably did so using the manuscript's rough descriptions for guidance, perhaps combined with unacknowledged reference to other published descriptions and illustrations of 'similar' exotic locales, rather than relying on any direct experience of their own with the subject matter.[1]

In some other places, blank spaces appear in the manuscript between entries for no apparent reason and were perhaps places that Van den Broecke intended to fill (at some later date) with new daily entries.

Toponyms are presented in the translation exactly as Van den Broecke wrote them, and modern equivalents are provided in square brackets. Note that Van den Broecke frequently varied his spellings and article constructions of a single toponym (e.g. Capbo Verde, Cabo Verde, Capo Verde). There are a few African exceptions to this editorial convention: variations of 'Grijncust', 'Goudcust', and 'Gunea' are always translated in the text as 'Grain Coast', 'Gold Coast', and 'Guinea' respectively; and the reader is trusted to interpret Capbo/Cabo/Capo Verde as Cape Verde, with confidence. In similar fashion, names for European countries have been presented in translation, rather than in Van den Broecke's Dutch spellings. The decision to preserve the original spellings of African toponyms was informed by arguments that these names themselves are valuable historical sources.[2]

Personal names are also presented as Van den Broecke wrote them, i.e., with inconsistent spellings. Note that at the time of Van den Broecke's voyages, most Dutch parents named their children according to a patronymic system, wherein children were known as their father's children; this is the '-son' meaning of the second names Van den Broecke rendered '-sen'. In modern Dutch

[1] Jones, *Zur Quellenproblematik der Geschichte Westafrikas*, pp. 99–105; Jones, 'Drink Deep, or Taste Not: Thoughts in the Use of Early European Records in the Study of African Material Culture'. Cf. Iselin, 'Reading Pictures: On the Value of the Copperplates in the *Beschryvinghe* of Pieter de Marees (1602) as Source Material for Ethnohistorical Research'.

[2] Stephen Bühnen, 'Place Names as an Historical Source'.

convention, the suffix '-zoon' is abbreviated as '-z'. Only under the Napoleonic régime in the Netherlands did all Dutch citizens adopt surnames.

Ship names are given in italics and without translation, i.e., with inconsistent spellings.

Non-Dutch words are also presented as Van den Broecke used them. This is, of course, an imperfect strategy because it is the nature of language to assimilate foreign terms, and this certainly was the case for early seventeenth-century Dutch, which was a language not yet standardized in any sense. Most of these 'foreign' words are maritime Portuguese, though some are of African, Arabic, and Indonesian origin. I employ this editing style to give some indication of the manuscript's composition and historical significance (e.g. to illustrate that a form of Portuguese was the trading and maritime *lingua franca* on the West African coast and Van den Broecke spoke it competently; unique African names for African products and political titles; and the introduction into the Dutch language of Indonesian words that describe maritime activity). All of these 'foreign' words appear in this edition in italics; each is explained in annotation on its first use, while subsequent uses are left in italics, but without notes.

Some Dutch words that defy translation into English are likewise given in italics and are explained in notes at their first appearance.

I have tried to limit the cross-referencing of Van den Broecke's observations on African matters to only those authors whose travels were nearly contemporary to his. Modern critical editions of the journals of Dierick Ruiters,[1] Johann von Lübelfing,[2] Pieter de Marees,[3] Adreas Ulsheimer,[4] Samuel Brun,[5] and Andrew Battel[6] are particularly valuable in this regard.

Van den Broecke began each day-entry with the same formula, 'den Xe ditto', which translates as 'On the Xth of the same (month)'. While it would have been possible to position these calendar checks as introductory adverbial phrases before the sentence proper, I have instead separated them from the sentence. I elected to do this to make the text less tortuous to read; Van den Broecke filled long sentences with a great many dependent descriptive phrases

[1] Naber, *Toortse der Zee-Vaert door Dierick Ruiters (1623).*

[2] Jones, *German Sources for West African History*, pp. 9–17.

[3] Naber, *Pieter de Marees, Beschryvinghe ende Historische verhael, van het Gout Koninckrijck van Gunea*; also Van Dantzig and Jones, *Pieter de Marees, Description and Historical Account of the Gold Kingdom of Guinea (1602).*

[4] Jones, *German Sources*, pp. 18–43.

[5] Naber, *Samuel Brun's Schiffarten (1624)*; Jones, *German Sources*, pp. 44–96.

[6] Ravenstein, *The Strange Adventures of Andrew Battel in Angola and the Adjoining Regions.*

which tend to confuse the modern reader. This composition style, which now seems so clumsy, indicates two significant attributes of the document. First, that it was written by a marginally literate person who had only a rudimentary education. Second, that the document aimed to impress a small Africana book-buying group of professors, clergy, merchants and magistrates with an over-wrought, pompous style.[1]

In a similar vein, I have divided some very long, compound sentences which contained multiple independent clauses into their shorter constituent parts.

At the bottom of every page of the manuscript are written the first few words that appear on the top of the next page. All of these repeated phrases have been deleted.

Van den Broecke wrote the month and year at the top of each page. Where these are redundant, they have been deleted.

Maps

Several maps are appended to the text. Four of them outline Van den Broecke's four trade voyages, and three others represent in more detail the principal African regions which he visited.

Transcription

Ratelband's transcription is near-perfect and is widely available in the Linschoten Society series at major academic libraries, and elsewhere through inter-library loan requests. Interested readers may check for themselves the translation I offer here.

Source References and Bibliography

I have consulted numerous language reference works, most notably: *Van Dale Groot woordenboek Nederlands-Engels* (Utrecht: Van Dale Lexicografie, 1991); P. G. J. van Sterkenburg, *Een glossarium van zeventiende-eeuws Nederlands* (Groningen: H. D. Tjeenk Willink, 1975); *Woordenboek der Nederlandsche Taal*, 29 vols and supplements ('s-Gravenhage and Leiden: 1882–1998).

[1] Van den Boogaart, 'Books on Black Africa: The Dutch Publications and their Owners in the Seventeenth and Eighteenth Centuries', pp. 118–19.

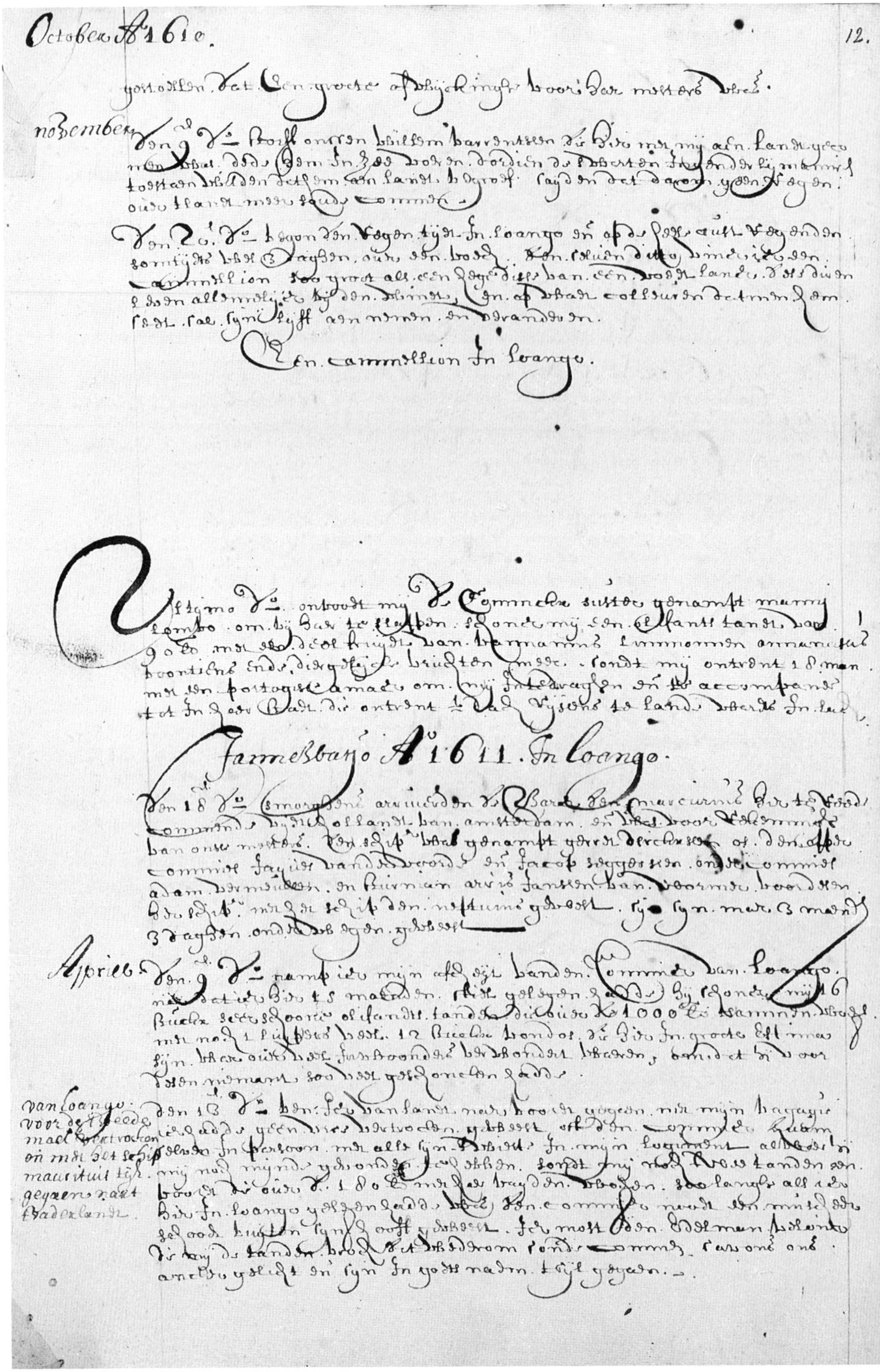

A sample page of the manuscript, f. 12r, entries for 11 September 1610 to 13 April 1611.

Journal of My Voyages to Capbo Verde [=Cape Verde], and from there to Guinea, and then Angola, and from there to the East Indies, under the command of the Honourable Governor-General Gerart Reynst, beginning in November 1605

In the year of our God and Saviour Jesus Christ, when we wrote 1605, in the month of November, I took a position as junior factor on a voyage from Doort [= Dordrecht] to Capbo Verde, earning twenty guilders[1] per month.[2]

the 16th day. In the evening I left Amsterdam for Doort [= Dordrecht], and left the service of the honourable, pious merchant Sr. Bartholomes Moor,[3] whom I had served for a period of three years.

the 23rd day. I arrived with the ship at Den Briel [= Briel], to sail with the first favourable wind that God should provide. The ship is named the *Roode Hart*, in size eighty lasts,[4] armed with eight half

[1] The guilder (Dutch *gulden*) is the Dutch unit of account; it is abbreviated as 'fl.' (*florin*), and is divided into twenty *stuivers*, or (in Van den Broecke's time) 320 *penningen*.

[2] This trip was made on behalf of Elias Trip's company; see the Introduction, p. 6. From the late 16th century, Dutch traders developed a commodity trade in hides, and in particular cowhides, from sahelian (desert-edge) West Africa. In response, local herders may have increased their stocks of large 'zebu' cattle in this era (Brooks, *Landlords and Strangers*, p. 139).

[3] This Antwerp-born merchant conducted his business from Amsterdam on the Herengracht, in a building known as 'the Moor'; see Elias, *De Vroedschap van Amsterdam*, I, pp. 307–8. This house's façade probably boasted a Moorish head, to distinguish it from others, as Dutch homes were not numbered until the Napoleonic period in the 19th century.

[4] A 'last' measured the carrying capacity of ships (similar to the English 'tonnage') and was roughly equivalent to two English tons or 120 cubic feet of shipping space. The unit 'last' was also used in the bulk trade in grains and salt, where

schackers,[1] six *steenstucken*,[2] and twenty-five men, and provisioned for a year. The chief factor was named Ewoudt Hendrickxssen[3] and the master[4] was Paulus Theunissen of Rotterdam.

the 30th day. With our ship as admiral,[5] we made a convoy to sail together to the Canary Islands – because of the freebooters[6] – with the master Pieter Cornelissen Spelman of Rotterdam,[7] who was also bound for Cabo Verde, and with master Pieter Cornelissen Uil, who

---

its weight or volume varied according to locality and each commodity (Posthumus, *Inquiry into the History of Prices in Holland*, p. lii; Boxer, *The Dutch Seaborne Empire*, p. 305; Jones, *Brandenburg Sources for West African History*, p. 316).

[1] Iron cannon firing shot of 5 to 6 *ponden* (= 2.5 to 3 kg.).

[2] *Steenstucken* were armaments of composite metallurgy first designed to fire breech-loaded stone shot *(steen)*, but later muzzle-loaded with either iron projectiles, such as small balls, expanding bar shot, and Langrel shot, or with munitions, including lit grenades and exploding wooden-canister shot filled with iron scrap (Van Dantzig and Jones, *Pieter de Marees*, p. 118 n.6; Green, *The Loss of the VOC Retourschip Batavia*, pp. 25–60).

[3] Ewoudt Hendricksz was mentioned in Van Wassenaer (*Historisch verhael*, June 1624: f. 91v) as a factor aboard the ship the *Swarte Leeuw*, of 180 lasts, 14 cannon, and 34 men. He had accumulated a cargo of 2,000 hides and some ambergris, red dye-wood, tobacco, elephant's tusks during nine months and eleven days on the coast, but died just a few days before the ship departed for home. See Van den Broecke's encounter with him in the journal entry for 5 January 1612.

[4] Throughout the manuscript, Van den Broecke uses the term *schipper*, which I have translated as 'master'. The (anglophone) term 'skipper' strictly refers only to the masters of small craft, and the title 'captain' was reserved in Dutch usage for commanders of military vessels of the Netherlands' fleet.

[5] In such convoys, ships were assigned these leadership roles of admiral, vice-admiral, and third-in-command (Asaert, *et al.*, *Maritieme Geschiedenis der Nederlanden*, II, pp. 124–5).

[6] Dutch merchant ships feared attack and seizure by privately-owned Portuguese, Spanish, and French warships, which they considered to be pirates (Dutch, *vrijbuiters*). Dutch ships were particularly vulnerable while in the Channel and along the Iberian coast, where enemy ships were plentiful and these 'freebooters' were under more careful metropolitan scrutiny. Once Dutch merchant ships arrived in West Africa, however, where Europeans' strict obedience to metropolitan orders was secondary to their eagerness for private enrichment, they could pursue peaceful trade and co-operation with people who were their 'enemy' in Europe. On the other hand, Europeans in West Africa could equally disregard peace treaties forged in European capitals, and instead opportunistically attack and seize foreign ships, cargoes and crew.

[7] Ratelband suggested that this Pieter Cornelissen Speelman was very probably the brother of Jan Cornelis Speelman, thus making him the uncle of Cornelis

was headed towards the West Indies to buy tobacco, and of whom we were also admiral. Before sunset we sailed together out to sea to undertake the voyages we were hired to do. May God bless us with luck and a safe voyage.

December [1605]

the first day. In the morning at sunrise we all passed by the Hoofden.[1]

the 5th day. We estimated the Sorles [= Scilly Isles] to be about five or six miles[2] from us. The wind was westerly, with a hard storm.

the 6th day. In the morning we consulted with each other and decided we would all run into Vaelmuyden [= Falmouth], because the storm stayed rough. But when night began to fall and it was too late to reach in the aforementioned harbour, we all put our ships about. And putting about in the winds of the bad storm we lost our fore-sail. And by the time we had set a new one, we were so close to the cliffs of Leser [= Lizard] that we could have shot at them with a *goetelinck*.[3] And had Almighty God suddenly given us a westerly wind, we would have hit them. At sunset we saw two ships being wrecked there, from which neither cat nor dog [= nobody] came. Well, we lost each other during the night.

the 7th day. Late at night we came to lay before the harbour of Dortmuyden [= Dartmouth], anchored at seventeen fathoms, close to shore.

Jansz Speelman, who became Governor-General of the Dutch East Indies (Ratelband, *Reizen naar West-Afrika*, p. 4 n. 1).

[1] The Dutch gave this name, meaning 'the Heads', to the passage between the cliffs of Dover and Calais (Van Dantzig and Jones, *Pieter de Marees*, p. 245 n.13).

[2] The 17th-century Dutch mile was equal to approximately 4 English miles, or 6.5 kilometres (Jones, *German Sources*, p.6; but see also Boxer, *The Dutch Seaborne Empire*, p. 305, who puts the 'very variable' Dutch mile at 3 English miles, or a 'league'). See also the appendix on 'Weights, Measures'.

[3] The term *goeteling* (from the Dutch verb *gieten*, 'to cast') refers to cast, rather than forged, small artillery pieces, twelve-pounder guns, which were usually mounted on ships but could be taken into the field (Van Dantzig and Jones, *Pieter de Marees*, p. 92 n. 8).

the 8th day. In the morning we were warped into the harbour between the two castles.

the 18th day. We sailed again out of the harbour of Doortmuyden [= Dartmouth], in the company of Moyen Arriaen, a master from Vlissinghen [= Vlissingen], on the ship named the *Tiger*, I mean rather, the *Luypaert*. They wanted to sail with us to Capo Verde and from there on to the West Indies. God Almighty bless us with a successful and safe journey.

January 1606

the 10th day. We passed the islands of the Canaries.

Arrived, for the first time, at Capo Verde, with the ship the *Roode Hart* from Doort [=Dordrecht]

the 15th day. In the morning we spotted the island[1] of Cabo Verde before us, lying south-east from us at four or five miles. From there we coasted alongside the shore, and encountered a reef which runs from the cape straight out to sea for about a half mile or a little bit less. This aforementioned reef lies at the north end, or northern point, of Capbo Verde. On the south side lies an island [= ?Ilets Madeleines[2]] about one and half miles out to sea. The outermost edge of the reef and island lie south-east and north-west from each other, at a distance of about three miles. Here our factor caught thirteen or fourteen beautiful, large rock bream. In the evening we anchored leeward of the island [= ?Gorée], between two ships. The first was the boat of Pieter Cornelissen Spelman and its yacht, which had left the Maas [river, in Zuid-Holland] with us, and who had arrived there the previous day.

[1] The 'island' they sighted may refer to the outermost end of the Cape Verde peninsula, which appeared to those aboard ship to be separated by water from the mainland. In Portuguese texts of the time, the 'island of Cape Verde' (Port., *Ilha do Cabo Verde*) often indicated the island of Santiago, in the Cape Verdes, but that does not seem to be what Van den Broecke refers to here.

[2] The island mentioned here, and perhaps also in the following sentence, was probably one of the dung-splattered islands known to the Dutch mariners as the 'Bescheeten Eilanden'. See also De Marees's description of the islands (Van Dantzig and Jones, *Pieter de Marees*, p. 10, with n. 2).

the 16th day. From ashore the *alcayer*[1] came aboard to collect his *dadecus* [= dash[2]] or customs duties. Following the law of the land we gave him five iron bars, two strings of crystals of size six, a ten-count of *carniseris*,[3] three bottles of brandy, with 4,000 *conteryen*,[4] or small beads.

the 18th day. In the morning I went with our factor aboard a *cachschuydt* [= lighter[5]] for Portodaele [= Portudal[6]], the most important trading place on the entire coast. Found three English ships

Arrived at Portodalle [=Portudal]

[1] Portuguese *alcaide*, 'governor, commandant', from Arabic and Wolof *al qâid*, 'the chief'. The *alcaide* resided in the village now called Dakar, and was appointed by the ruler of Cayor. Europeans paid anchorage dues here, where they could anchor their large ships in deep waters close to shore; smaller ships were then dispatched to the shallow anchorages at Portudal and Joal (Brooks, *Landlords and Strangers*, p. 205). Van den Broecke's outfit may have overpaid their anchorage dues: after De Marees visited here in c.1601, he remarked that the *alcaide* usually charged a toll of 'three bars of iron, but from those who do not know their customs, they take as much as they can' (Van Dantzig and Jones, *Pieter de Marees*, p. 12, with n. 9). See also Ruiters (Naber, *Toortse der Zee-Vaert*, p.51), and Van Wassenaer (*Historisch verhael*, June 1624: ff. 91v–92r) who recorded *alcaides* at Rufisque, Portudal and Joal.

[2] The ubiquitous West African term 'dash' is of uncertain etymology, perhaps deriving from the Portuguese words *dação*, 'donation', or *doacão* , 'present', or from other, African words. For more detail see De Marees's chapter on the subject (Van Dantzig and Jones, *Pieter de Marees*, ch. 10).

[3] From the Portuguese word, *carneiras*, 'sheepskins'.

[4] From the Portuguese word, *conterias*, 'pearls'. Here they are beads, as Van den Broecke himself indicates. On the wide variety of size and colours of different types of beads traded on the Petite Côte at this time, see Alvares de Almada (Hair, *André Alvares de Almada*, p. 24).

[5] European traders typically used combinations of large and small ships. The larger, main ships were capable of ocean travel and served as floating warehouses which supported smaller, light-draft sailing craft which were more suitable to coastal and riverine shallows. Often the smaller ships would be prefabricated in Europe, carried aboard the main vessels, and then assembled on the African beaches (Gorée island was often used for this purpose); for examples, see entries for 7 May 1606 and 17 January 1612.

[6] Portudal, on the Senegalese coast south of Cape Verde and Rufisque, was a principal port town of the Serer state of Bawol. Here and elsewhere on the 'Petite Côte', Dutch merchants tapped the existing commercial networks through Portuguese 'New Christian' (Port., *cristãos novos*) and Luso-African intermediaries, who were involved in the coastal traffic in salt and fish and the sea trade with Portuguese Atlantic islands in hides and wine. The local traders

here, lying at anchor and trading. In the evening there came yet another English ship to the roadstead.[1]

the 20th day. We brought our trade-goods ashore. The factor rented a house with a black woman to serve me for two iron bars per month.[2] We paid our tolls and customs together to the factor, so that we were allowed to trade here, besides other traders, which amounted to fifty-seven iron bars, sixteen bottles of brandy, eighteen ten-counts of *carniseris*, nine shirts, nine hats,[3] nine rapiers,[4] 36,000 *conteryes* or beads. The chief factor went immediately back aboard and left me there ashore with our constable Jan Pieterssen van Sweden to trade.

the 23rd day. For the first time, I traded for thirty-six hides at the rate of two [hides] per bar. The same day, such great numbers of red grasshoppers flew over Portodaele [= Portudal] that in some places one could hardly see the sky, and this lasted for more than two glasses [= one hour]. They were as follows: red in colour and at least a thumb's thickness and a finger's length. This year was such a dire time that parents were forced to sell their children for their subsistence and maintenance.[5]

---

also accessed overland markets in slaves, gold, and kola (Boulègue, *Les Luso-africains de Sénégambie*; Curtin, *Economic Change in Precolonial Africa*, pp. 95–109). In daily entries below, it is evident that Dutch companies were posting resident factors ashore to buy and bulk cargoes for export.

[1] On the English trade at Cape Verde at the turn of the century, see De Moraes, 'Le Commerce des peaux à la Petite Côte au XVIIe siècle'.

[2] Van den Broecke apparently remained ashore for the next five months (until the entry for 6 June 1606).

[3] De Marees noted that elite men distinguished themselves by wearing long cotton shirts and caps (Van Dantzig and Jones, *Pieter de Marees*, p. 11).

[4] Rapiers (long, slender, and double-edged) were something of an unusual import, compared to the broad, single-edged halberds and billhooks typically used in African warfare and agriculture.

[5] See also Van den Broecke's description below, in the section on 'Manners and Customs' of this journal. Subsistence crises recurred throughout the century, with severe disasters occurring at least every decade; see the chronology in Becker, 'Notes sur les conditions écologiques en Sénégambie'. These crises exposed the most vulnerable members of Senegambian communities, that is children and women, to enslavement. For descriptions of locust plagues in the late 16th century, see Alvares de Almada (Hair, *André Alvares de Almada*, p. 21).

February 1606

the 2nd day. We entered into a contract[1] with the Rotterdammer, Pieter Cornelissen Spelman, and combined together our trade-goods and cargoes so as to not spoil the market. It was also agreed that Pieter Cornelissen Spelman would sail home with all of the hides that were traded in the next month.

The same day our chief factor paid the tolls and customs to the king of Juwaelle [= Joal[2]], which comprised eighteen bars of iron, ten hats, ten shirts, ten rapiers, twelve bottles of brandywine, three ten-counts of *carniseris*, and two strands of size eighteen crystal.

the 9th day. A French freebooter arrived here at the roadstead. The captain was named Cavallion. Our sloop tried to sail next to it, in order to take it, but they sailed too fast for it. The French ship immediately set sail again and left for the West Indies.

the 27th day. A French ship arrived here also at Portodael [= Portudal], the captain of which was named Pierre le Noor, from Diepen [= Dieppe] who came here to trade.

March [1606]

the 20th day. Two Portuguese barks arrived from Sante Domningo [= São Domingos, Buguendo[3]], loaded with hides, elephant's tusks, wax,[4] ambergris,[5] and other such merchandise.

the 25th day. I reported home via a French ship from Diepen

[1] This 'contract' was probably a price-fixing agreement among the Dutch ships.

[2] Joal was the principal coastal trade town of the Serer state of Siin (Brooks, *Landlords and Strangers*, p. 204).

[3] The town of Buguendo (the Portuguese 'São Domingos') lay inland, on a tributary of the Cacheu River (Ibid., pp. 92–3).

[4] The Dutch traders, unlike their Portuguese counterparts, took an interest in the wax trade. Prior to the development of Dutch trade in the late 16th century, Wolof honey gatherers discarded most of the beeswax from their combs (Ibid., p.139).

[5] Ambergris is waxy concretion produced in the intestines of whales. The insoluble remains of carcases were washed ashore, where they were collected and sent back to the Netherlands for use in cooking and making perfumes.

[= Dieppe], which was leaving the coast. The captain was named Thomas Rossel. He was leaving here with two ships all in all. The other captain was named Barbauw,[1] and they left the coast with more than 16,000 hides, a number of elephant's tusks and ambergris from the coast.

the 29th day. I went to the house of a Portuguese mulatto, by the name of Anthoni de Moor,[2] where I bought dinner.[3]

May [1606]

the first day. A French ship with its yacht, both sent by the governor of Habel de Grasse [= Le Hâvre de Grace], arrived leeward of the island of Capo Verde, and they let it be known that they wanted to seize all of the English and Dutch [ships] that were there on the coast.[4]

the 5th day. Our ship came, with just eleven men on it, from Refusco [= Rufisque[5]] to here, before Portodaele [= Portudal], so as to not be

[1] Van den Broecke also encountered a sloop at Portudal which belonged to a 'French captain named Barbu' on his next voyage to Africa; see entry below for 3 February 1608. Could there be some familial relationship between this Barb(a)u(w) and the famous West African chronicler Jean Barbot (1655–1712), author of *A Description of the Coasts of North and South Guinea* (1732)? (see Hair, Jones, and Law, *Barbot on Guinea*, I, pp. ix–xviii).

[2] Perhaps this was the same Anthoni de Moor (also De Morias) whom Van den Broecke recorded later as having found employment in the East Indies (Coolhaas, *Pieter van den Broecke in Asië*, pp. 77, 77 n. 6).

[3] De Marees noticed that Portuguese on this part of the coast traded freely with merchants of other many other nations (Van Dantzig and Jones, *Pieter de Marees*, p. 12).

[4] These French freebooters threatened English ships despite the Treaty of London (1604), which made peace between England and Iberia (and its client, France). The English interpreted this treaty as allowing them access to South Atlantic trade, but the Iberians disagreed, and thus hostilities (as well as peaceful trade) between the two empires persisted in this area; see Hair and Law, 'The English in Western Africa to 1700', pp. 247–50. French threats to Dutch ships were to be expected, as the Netherlands and Iberia were still at war, at least until the Twelve Years' Truce began in 1609. Dutch and English sea merchants were perhaps predisposed to allying with each other in the face of such threats, as they had been formally allied against the Iberians until the Treaty of London was signed.

[5] Originally known as Rio Fresco, as it was a place where many European ships took on fresh water. On the history of the name, see Mauny, 'Notes d'histoire de Rufisque'.

taken immediately by the Frenchmen by surprise. It [=our ship] was joined by the four English ships, which offered us total support, as they had heard that the Frenchman boasted that they had shot at and sunk an English ship which had been loaded with pilchards and was bound for the Straits [of Gibraltar].

the 7th day. The aforementioned Frenchman arrived with his yacht and a sloop, which they had put together on the island [= Gorée].[1] He set his anchor close to ours and thought that he was alongside us, but his cable broke and he passed us and ended up right between us and the English ships. The ship was about 150 lasts in size, armed with fourteen light metal pieces and 180 men. They then sent their lieutenant to board us and the English ships, to ask if there wasn't someone who had some victuals to sell him. We answered him that we had only powder and lead. They immediately lifted anchor and sailed out to sea, we thought for the West Indies.

June [1606]

the 6th day. I went from Portudaele [= Portudal] with a sloop full of hides to Juwaele [= Joal], to our chief factor who had been trading there. On coming there, I found our large sloop loaded with hides, elephant's tusks, and wax [and] with which I immediately sailed for our ship, arriving there on the 8th day of this month.

Sailed with a ship full of hides, from Portodaelle [=Portudal] to Juwalle [=Joal]

the 16th day. We spotted two sails coming in from sea, sailing to the roadstead leeward of the island. By night time, they came to anchor by us.

the 18th day. In the morning before sunrise we had our first *travoade*,[2] which lasted for about half an hour, with terrible lightning and thunder. After the rain stopped, our master went aboard the two French freebooters to see from whence they had come. He discovered that one was a small French ship from Honfloer [= Honfleur] and the other was a Portuguese caravel they had taken near the Canary Islands. The French captain told our master that they had

Had the first *travado* at Cabo Verde

[1] See p. 27, n.5.

[2] *Travoado* is a common 17th-century Dutch spelling of the Portuguese *trovoado*, 'a hard, sudden storm.'

a commission from the Prince, His Excellency Mauritius of Nassau – whereupon our master returned, 'Then why aren't you flying his flag?' Finally, once our master had returned aboard, he sent me aboard the aforementioned French ship to invite the captain and his crew to come aboard our ship to visit, and once they had come aboard and had eaten and drunk, our master would ask to see their commission. Thus confronted, the French, who were at least five men for every one of ours, fell into their boats together and rowed off – and not without great peril from being shot and sunk, as the master let fire two rounds from half *sackers*. We immediately lifted our anchor and began to sail towards them. But seeing us under sail, they immediately cut their anchors and escaped, as they were better sailed than us. From our ship two rounds were fired through the small French ship, and the cannonball could be seen hitting the water on the other side [of their ship]. Three Frenchmen fell dead (as we found out later). Finally, as night was upon us and we saw that the French sailed too fast for us, we sailed again to the Refusco [= Rufisque] roadstead.

the 22nd day. Now that our goods had been traded, we sailed leeward of the island of Cabo Verde [= ?Gorée] in the company of Pieter Cornelissen Spelman, and once we had supplied ourselves with firewood and water, we would sail home together.

the 26th day. We dropped anchor by the two English ships, the commander over both of which was a Mister Johan Hillis, who wanted to spend the coming rainy season trading.[1] We decided, as we were ready, to go to sail in the evening in the company of master Pieter Cornelissen Spelman of Rotterdam. Shortly afternoon, an English sloop coming from Juwale [= Joal] arrived near us, which brought us news that there sat before Juwaele [= Joal] a large Lübick [= Lübeck]

[1] The rainy season at Cape Verde begins in late June and continues through the middle of August. The *trovoado* mentioned above (entry for 18 June 1606) was the harbinger of the rainy season's imminent onset. European traders typically scheduled their journeys to coincide with the dry season, which was both relatively healthier and saw heightened African commercial activity, owing to dry transportation routes and freedom from agricultural labours (Brooks, *Landlords and Strangers*, pp. 174–7).

ship, loaded with sugar.[1] We immediately raised our anchors and sailed there.

the 27th day. In the mid-morning of this day we saw the aforementioned Lübick ship anchored before Juwaelle [= Joal]. We came to rest beside it, and Pieter Cornelissen Spelman was on the bow, and demanded their surrender or else we would take them by force, to which they most readily agreed, promising to do so [= surrender] on the condition that the master could keep his cargo and ship, and the mates could keep their plunder. Then the chief boatswain, who was the only officer besides the recorder to still be alive, implored us to first fire five or six shots over their ship, so that if they returned to Lissebonne [= Lisbon] they could report what had happened. [We agreed] to do it. But when our master ordered the constable to fire three or four shots, overshooting and missing them, he [the constable] thought he heard him say 'hitting them'. So the first shot went right through the ship, shooting off a black man's shoulder and a black woman's heel. Both of them immediately died. In short, the ship was surrendered to us.

A Lübick ship windward of Juwalle, [=Joal] coming from Ste. Thome [=São Tomé] and bound for Lisbonna [=Lisbon]

This ship was 120 lasts in size, loaded with sugar from Ste. Thome [= São Tomé], seven bales of cotton, and a number of elephant tusks, and which was coming from Ste. Thome and headed for Lisbonna [= Lisbon]. [The ship] was from Lübick [= Lübeck], with a master named Jacop Hollander, who had died, as had seventeen of his principal officers, so that there were just eleven Easterners [= Baltic men] still living, among them the chief boatswain and recorder.

This ship was chartered by the Portuguese. They had been under way for five months and had suffered much hunger and distress. There also were four Portuguese, with at least ninety slave men and women, who were so skinny that it was astonishing. Sent the Portuguese ashore, according to their request, with an English boat from the captain Mister Liefkens, and thirteen slaves. The plunder was

[1] That is a ship from the 'neutral' town of Lübeck, in Germany, which carried a Spanish or Portuguese passport to haul sugar from the island of São Tomé, off the West African coast, to Lisbon, via a refreshing stop in Joal. German ships were indeed a rare sight in African waters in this early part of the century (Naber, *Pieter de Marees*, pp. lxv–lxvi).

divided by our men with around 3,000 *realen van achten*,[1] and some gold chains which the recorder Manuwel Lauw, a Lübick [=Lübeck] man by birth but who resided in Lisabon [= Lisbon], claimed to be his. There was a sack of 1,000 *realen van achten* missing, which had presumably had been pilfered by the Englishmen upon boarding.

the 30th day. We lifted our anchors together and sailed along the coast towards the island of Cabo Verde [= Gorée].

July [1606]

the 7th day. We arrived leeward of the aforementioned island.

the 8th day. Our chief factor rewarded the Englishman, who had alerted us, with all of the black men and women, on the condition that he would give us some *manimentos*[2] and fetch us water.[3]

the 16th day. In the morning we raised anchor, and the three of us[4] formed a convoy to sail home. May Almighty God let us arrive safely at our destination.

August [1606]

the 27th day. In the morning we spotted the peak of Ste Jorge [= of the Azores] and estimated that it was eighteen to twenty miles away.

[1] The Portuguese unit of account was the *real* (plural *réis*, with amounts normally recorded with a $-symbol denoting thousands). A piece of eight was a coin worth 8 *réis* (Van Dantzig and Jones, *Pieter de Marees*, p.194 n. 3). Thus, the plundered coins totalled about 24$000 *réis*.

[2] Portuguese *manimentos*, 'victuals'.

[3] This English interest in slaves is surprising, as (after the venture of John Hawkins in the 1560s, which was not sustained) English ships did not carry slaves to the Americas until the 1630s (at the earliest), when sugar cultivation took root on Barbados. This English ship probably hoped to sell these slaves locally, on the Petite Côte, to another European vessel which was bound for the Americas. That they would have carried these slaves to Europe is regarded as less likely, although an English ship seized in a Spanish port in 1608 after having left Senegambia may have had a cargo of slaves: for a discussion of the evidence for English slaving in this period, see Hair, 'Attitudes to Africans in English Primary Sources on Guinea to 1650'.

[4] That is, Van den Broecke's ship, the *Roode Hart*, Speelman's ship, and the captured prize.

the 28th day. We spotted the island Tersera [= Terceira] and, in the evening at sunset, the island of Ste Michiel [= São Miguel]. We got a fierce *trovoado* with rain and terrible thunderclaps and lightning and as a result were blown away from the others.

the 29th day. This morning, before midday, we found the others.

October 1606

the 3rd day. In the morning we reached land near Goere [= Goeree Overflakkee[1]]. Seven or eight pilots came aboard. They had been sent by captain Sijbrandt Vijdt to bring into port a Spanish galleon that he had captured. We had to give them each four Flemish pounds in piloting fees. Shortly after noon we arrived safely on the river Maas. The prize [ship] went with Pieter Cornelissen towards Rotterdam, and we went with our ship towards Doort [= Dordrecht], where we dropped anchor on Saturday.

Arrived home at the Maas with the ship the *Hart*, thanks to God, from Capo Verde

the 14th day. I went from Doort [= Dordrecht] via Dorgouw [= Tergouw, Gouda] to Amsterdam, where I found my parents and friends, all doing well. My father lived in the rear residence at Engellenborch [= Engelenburg]. My oldest sister Margrita was in Layden [= Leiden] married to Johannes, the eldest son of Rector Swardecroon.[2] May Almighty God grant them happiness.

Manners and Life of the Blacks of Cabo Verde

The natives here are pitch black, large in stature, bad-natured, and clever in all of their affairs, and terribly thievish. Many speak French, as there are always Frenchmen here.[3] Some speak good English and a

[1] Goeree is a small island at the shallow mouth of the river Maas (in the province of Zuid-Holland).

[2] Swardecroon was rector of the prestigious Latin School in Leiden.

[3] De Marees indicated that fewer and fewer French ships were coming to the coast at the time when he was there, c. 1601 (Van Dantzig and Jones, *Pieter de Marees*, pp.10–11).

few speak our *Duytsse*[1] language, even though our countrymen visit there more often than the English.

The majority are Mohammedans. The rest pray to the moon and some to the Devil, whom they call Cammate.[2] When asked why they pray to the Devil, they give the answer, 'we know well that there is a God, who made heaven and earth, and he does not harm us. But Cammate does us harm night and day.' And often they are wizards, too.

They are very clever in wars against their neighbours. When they go to war, they have as their weapons: a broad, large assegai [= lance, spear] made as a halberd, and with five to seven small assegais. And they have a bow with a quiver full of poisoned arrows, which they know how to use well enough.

Anyone who is taken prisoner from time to time, by them or their enemies, is made into a slave forever, even when he is a great nobleman. These people have an unusual custom (of which I approve) that they will not go anywhere unarmed, even if it is just ten steps away.

They also know how to ride horses: I saw a servant of the king of Lambaja [= Lambaay[3]] (who lives about eighteen miles inland) who gave his mount the spurs and threw an assegai out of his hand into the air, and then caught it in flight with such a unique quickness that it was amazing. Their horses come mostly from the Senega[l] River, where the Moors of Barbayen [= Barbary] sell them.[4] They are

[1] Here, *Duytsse* means 'Dutch' (as it also does in the Netherlands' national anthem, 'Wilhelmus'), and not the modern Dutch *Duits(e)*, meaning 'German'.

[2] See also the remarks of Tilleman in the late 17th century (Winsnes, *Erick Tilleman*, p. 9): 'They worship the Devil, whom they call Commaté, and make sacrifices to him.' Father Alexis de Saint-Lô similarly identified 'Camaté' as the devil, and described the 'people of Camaté' as a group in rebellion against the king of Bawol's high wartime taxes (Thilmans and De Moraes, 'Dencha Four, souverain de Baol', pp. 702–3).

[3] Lumbaay was the principal city of Bawol (Boulègue, *Le Grand Jolof*, pp. 21, 175–7).

[4] Arabian and Barbary horses were larger and therefore militarily superior to the native Senegambian pony breeds, but they were also susceptible to trypanosomiasis, which the ponies tolerated (Webb, *Desert Frontier*, ch. 4; Curtin, *Economic Change in Precolonial Africa*, pp. 221–3).

extremely fast. The tack is made in the English manner.[1] On the 25th of January 1606, I saw one of the king's servants who ran and passed a horse. This same black man took an assegai in his hand which he threw into the air, while running, and overtook it and caught it in flight.

The fishermen are also extraordinarily strong swimmers and able fishermen. The canoes are made out of a single tree,[2] and [they] go as a group in the mornings before sunrise with a land wind three or four miles out to sea to fish, until midday when the sea wind comes, and then they come in the same way back out from sea. Some have three sails above each other.[3] Their fishing tackle is hooks, wooden harpoons, [and] netted sacks which they fill with rocks and let sink down to bottom [and] with which they catch many fish, because they are so well and cleverly made. Here on the coast are found all sorts of beautiful and tasty fish, of which the locals consider a mess of sardines to be a delicacy. They roast them on coals without having gutted them, and eat them with their hands along with couscous made from *milli*[4] flour.

[1] English-style tack included bitted bridles and saddles with stirrups. The latter enabled riders to use the strength of their legs and torso to wield large weapons such as assegais with greater force and balance than a bareback rider could muster (Webb, *Desert Frontier*, pp. 71–2). Portuguese-made equestrian equipment, made in both European and Moorish styles, constituted a significant share of Portuguese merchants' sales in Senegambia (see Elbl, 'The Portuguese Trade with West Africa', pp. 407–8).

[2] Probably dug out from the tall bombax, or 'cotton', tree (*Bombax buonopozense*); see Brooks, *Landlords and Strangers*, p. 207.

[3] Senegambian fisherman probably adapted their dug-out pirogues to sea travel under sail, after they had served on Portuguese caravels (Brooks, ibid., pp. 209–10). For more detail on late 16th-century pirogue technology, see Alvares de Almada's description of the craft (Hair, *André Alvares de Almada*, p. 38); and for 17th-century fishing, see Barbot (Hair, *et al.*, *Barbot on Guinea*, I, pp. 71–2).

[4] *Millie* (and other spelling variations) denotes 'grain', including varieties of maize, millet and sorghum. For a discussion of the problems in identifying *millie*, see Hernæs, *Slaves, Danes and African Coast Society*, pp. 337–40; and Wigboldus, 'De oudste Indonesische maïscultuur', pp. 19–31. Ruiters described the entire process of making couscous on the Petite Côte (Naber, *Toortse der Zee-Vaert*, pp. 54–5). See also Barbot, who however probably based his description on Dapper's earlier (1668) account (Hair, *et al.*, *Barbot on Guinea*, I, pp. 122–3).

A man at Capo Verde in the city of Portodaele [=Portudal] drank a bottle of one and a half *mengel* brandy in one gulp

These people drink very strong stuff,[1] especially brandywine.[2] I have seen a man, named Coli, who downed in one gulp one of my bottles of one and half *mengel*[3] in size, and then asked for more. Their daily drink is palm wine and *wijn de po* which is boiled up [= fermented] from *milli*,[4] and on which they can get very drunk.

The men take as many women as they can keep, so that those of means normally have eight or nine wives, and they keep wives as their slaves. They must plough the land with hoes, which is heavy labour, and then seed and weed. So long as the man sits and eats, they must stand there to serve him. When he has finished they have to make do with the leftovers. I have seen there that women came out of country with twelve to sixteen hides on their head and a child tied to their back, on top of which they were in late pregnancy, and the man going beside them carrying nothing other than his weapon. The women are so strong in nature that as soon as they have given birth, they take the baby and walk with it into the sea or into a fountain to bathe; and then they come out and immediately come back to the bed of the man, and there is a particular caste or group in which the man beds down for eight to ten days as soon as the wife has given birth, who has to take care of her man, or else he will not sleep with her for some time.[5] Some women have such large breasts that they hang over their navels.

[1] *Dit volck drinckt seer starck toeback.* I believe that *toeback* means only 'stuff' here, and not 'tobacco'. Van den Broecke's phrase is certainly unusual but not totally unheard of in Dutch, and is akin to the old-fashioned German expression 'starker Toback', normally describing strong medicine. I cannot agree with the translation of this passage by Thilmans and De Moraes, 'Ces gens boivent de tabac très fort ...', nor their explanatory note, 'Boire est fréquemment utilisé à l'époque dans le sens de fumer' (Thilmans and De Moraes, 'Les Passages à la Petite Côte de Pieter van den Broecke', p. 487 n. 2).

[2] European merchants sold some small amounts of liquors (see entries for 16 January 1606; 20 January 1606; 2 February 1606), but much of the 'brandywine' consumed here was the Cape Verdian sugarcane brandy, *aguardente*. See also Ruiters (Naber, *Toortse der Zee-Vaert*, p. 50) on brandywine drinking on the Petite Côte.

[3] A *mengel* equals two pints, or 1.2 litres.

[4] This *wijn de po* must be a local beer, probably like the millet beer of the Gold and Slave Coasts, which the Dutch knew as *pito* (or *pitou*, *pitouw*).

[5] Van den Broecke's description of this practice, known in comparative anthropology as 'couvade', contrasts with other contemporary descriptions of Senegambia, which make no mention of this custom. Furthermore, Van den

Parents are sometimes forced to sell their children for food. During my stay I bought a lovely young girl of about ten years of age from her mother for the price of 130 lb of rice,[1] [and] the mother acted so coolly, as if it were not even her child. Various parents came to offer me the virginity of their children, aged seven or eight years, for a couple of handfuls of rice. These women are tremendously vain, especially about their teeth.

A young girl about 10 years old was bought from her mother for 132 lb of rice

When a friend dies, be they a man or a woman, the friends gather all together, big and small, and wail like mad dogs, [and this] continues for three or four days and nights. That being done, they bury him to the sound of pipes and drums, and set a pot of water near his head, to be changed every morning and evening, and some food, so that he should not suffer hunger or thirst on his journey, and they do this for a year and sometimes longer. Every evening the principal friends come to weep over the dead body, and continue to whoop under the influence of strong drink even five or six days after the deceased's death.[2]

The blacks strongly believe that their dead will turn white[3] and that they shall come with such ships as we have now to trade and visit their friends. But they do not want to let on, because they are rich.

Most of the men can weave with yarn which is spun by the old women. Here, they make handsome cloths and excellent blue dyed

---

Broecke probably misunderstood the motivations behind suspending sexual intercourse after childbirth (which remains a widespread practice in West Africa) when he described it as a punishment for wives' lack of attentiveness. Rather, a nursing mother risked her infant's health if she became pregnant again too quickly. See also Jobson's 17th-century description of this practice (Gamble and Hair, *Discovery of the River Gambra*, pp. 114–5, with 115 n. 1).

[1] Very little rice was grown in the immediate area (see Boulègue, *Le Grand Jolof*, p. 76). The rice mentioned here was probably brought from the moister regions to the south.

[2] European visitors were generally impressed by the emotion and duration of Senegambian funerals. Compare Van den Broecke's observations with Alvares de Almada's more extensive description (Hair, *André Alvares de Almada*, pp. 35–6).

[3] Hemmersam noted the same belief on the Gold Coast (Jones, *German Sources*, p.104). See also Ulsheimer, also referring to the Gold Coast (ibid., p.31).

ones.[1] The cloths are bought in good numbers by the Portuguese, and transported from here to Ste Dommingh [= São Domingos, Buguendo]. These cloths are also much desired on the coast of Guinea and are sold there for a *pese*[2] of gold. I had brought some of the cloths later to Loango, where I got an elephant's tusk weighing 88 lb for a single piece. Good soap and excellent earthen pots are also made here.

The following trade goods are found on the mainland of Capbo Verde

Great numbers of oxhides, which are lighter than those of the West Indies. During my time, there were more than 30,000 pieces per year, which includes some buffalo- and *hart*-hides,[3] and many eland hides. Furthermore, little gold is found here, but it is better than that on the Gold Coast. Elephant's tusks are also available for sale here, which come from the Gambia River. Wax, rice, and fine ambergris are available here as well, and which also comes mostly from the same Gambia River. During my time there in the year 1606, there was a piece of ambergris of 83 lb found in the Gambi[a] River. It was almost as big as a canoe. People say, and I believe, that it was thrown ashore by the sea. I bought a piece from this in Portodaele [= Portudal] [weighing] four Dutch lb for fourteen bars of iron per ounce.

[1] On differential gender roles in manufacturing cloth, see Carreira, *Panaria Cabo-Verdiano-Guineense*, p. 53; Duncan, *Atlantic Islands*, pp. 219–22. Senegambian dyers used true indigo (*Indigo tinctoria*), a crop probably acquired across the sudan (i.e. interior) area of West Africa as part of a complex also including Asian cotton (*Gossypium* sp) and the narrow loom. Van den Broecke's stay in Cape Verde coincided with the onset of a sustained drought on the Cape Verde islands, during which many weavers fled the islands for moister climes (Brooks, *Landlords and Strangers*, pp.164–6).

[2] A Portuguese *peça* , 'coin', was a non-minted, flattened piece of gold used as a currency in coastal West Africa (Van Dantzig and Jones, *Pieter de Marees*, p.194 n.5). Naber estimated the weight at 6.15 grams, and its value as fl. 8 (Naber, *Pieter de Marees*, pp. 19, 280).

[3] Here, the author probably means an antelope with horns.

The Portuguese control this river [= Gambia] and have many places where they trade alone.

Most of the Portuguese's and major trade is in Portodaelle [= Portudal] and, after that, in Juwaele [= Joal]. These [traders] are mostly exiles from Portugal. They gather here around 100 to 150 slaves, which they ship to Catsieuw [= Cacheu] or Ste. Domingho [= São Domingos, Buguendo],[1] and from there embark for the West Indies, where they gather together a great fortune from the slaves and then return, when they have been pardoned, to Portugal to retire.[2]

Price of the goods which I bought at Portodaele [=Portudal]

Ambergris, the best	14, 15, to 16 iron bars per ounce
the bad [ambergris]	10, 11 [bars]
elephant's tusks, two in a hundredweight	15, 16 bars per *quintal*[3]
small to average [size tusks]	[no price given]
wax	10, 11 bars per *quintal*
rice	2, 3 bars per *quintal*

[1] On the Portuguese and Luso-African trade forts on the Cacheu, see Duncan, *Atlantic Islands*, pp. 201–2, 214–15.

[2] A significant minority of the African-based Portuguese traders were *banidos* ('exiles') from Portugal. Such traders struggled to accumulate capital in the African economies in the form of slaves and then convert this human wealth into imperial currencies which could earn them pardons to return home. Most exiles never did return to Portugal; many simply perished, others were unsuccessful in their trades, some preferred to stay in Africa, and others migrated to Brazil but never returned to Portugal. On Luso-Africans' economic strategies in general, see Miller, *Way of Death*, pp. 246–51. On their slaving strategies particular to this coast in the early 17th century, see Ruiters (Naber, *Toortse der Zee-Vaert*, pp. 55–6).

[3] The Portuguese *quintal* (pl. *quintais*) was a unit of weight similar to the English and Dutch hundredweights, all of which contained roughly a hundred of their respective national poundweights. In the17th century the Dutch *pond* weighed almost 300 grams, making the '*quintal* of 120 Dutch lb' about 36 kg. or 80 lb (Jones, *Brandenburg Sources*, p. 318).

hides from the Portuguese	1, 1¼ per bar
[hides] from the locals[1]	2 and 1½, [but] sometimes, when there are few ships, which seldom happens, they give 3, 4, or 5 per iron bar.

[1] The difference in prices, between 'Portuguese' and local sellers, probably represents a preferential price paid to European agents, presumably to cover commissions or other expenses incurred. The difference might also, however, reflect hides from two different types of cattle: local, Serer herders tended the smaller, trypanosomiasis-tolerant West African shorthorn cattle, whereas Fula herders north of the tsetse zone had the larger 'zebu' cattle (Brooks, *Landlords and Strangers*, p. 215; Curtin, *Economic Change in Precolonial Africa*, pp. 218–21).

Journal of My Voyage for the first time to Angola, as Junior Factor with the ship the *Neptunnis,* ninety lasts in size, armed with ten *goetelingen,* six *steenstucken,* and thirty men, the master was Aris Janssen from Schans, and Harman Bitter was Senior Merchant

the 14th of November, 1607

that day. I went from Amsterdam to Texsel [= Texel] to sail with the first favourable wind that Almighty God should give.

[blank space in the manuscript]

the 26th day. We sailed in God's name with a north-east wind from Texssel [= Texel] in a convoy of about sixty ships. May Almighty God bless us with luck and a safe trip, amen.

December [1607]

First day. In the morning we decided to put into harbour in England because the wind blew against us, and we got a hard storm.

the 3rd day. In the evening we came before Vaelmuyden [= Falmouth] but could not come in there, because night was falling. Remained under sail therefore, throughout the night.

the 4th day. In the morning we put into Vaelmuyden [= Falmouth]. When you come in, there lies a reef you can safely pass around on either side. Once you are in, there lies a sandbar of about two fathoms, but we stayed before it and anchored at seven fathoms.

For the first time with the ship the *Neptunis* in Vaelmuyden [=Falmouth]

the 13th day. We went with a north-east wind again out to sea and then as soon as land was out of sight, the wind again turned against us with a hard storm.

the 15th day. For the second time we came into Vaelmuyden [= Falmouth]. As we weathered the cape, we saw a French ship there stranded ashore.

the 16th day. Again, more than twenty-five ships arrived there, in the harbour by us. Learned that during this storm, more than eight ships had wrecked and were stranded upon Engelandtseynde [= Land's End].

the 21st day. With a north-east wind, we raised our anchor before midday and went in God's name to sea for a second time.

January 1608

The first day. In the evening as the sun set, we thought we saw the island Portosande [= Porto Santo]. In the evening the wind blew contrary with a hard storm.

While at sea, our rudder is struck from the ship by a storm

the 5th day. During the day watch[1] our rudder was thrown from the ship by a deep wave, [and] then it hung only on the top hook. Thanks to God we could get it aboard. Found that for the two bottom rudder braces, I mean hooks, the gudgeons were eaten away and that the hooks remained stuck in the rudder braces. The others were also mostly worn-out and eaten away by the salt water. The storm continued just as hard.

the 6th day. We were busy trying to repair our rudder. We took a different tack and let ourselves drift about at God's mercy.

Sailed 25 miles in a day in the Spanish sea without a rudder

8th to 9th day. The storm and wind were the same [and] we were by reckoning around twelve to fifteen miles off the Portuguese coast. Set our *schover* sails[2] along with the *blinde*.[3] Went south-west without

[1] Dutch crews scheduled six watches, each of which lasted four hours. The day watch lasted from 4 A.M. to 8 A.M. (Thom, *Journal of Jan van Riebeck*, I, p. 4 n. 7; Asaert *et al.*, *Maritieme Geschiedenis der Nederlanden*, p. 139).

[2] The *schover* sails are the large sail and the fore-sail (Ratelband, *Reizen naar West-Afrika*, p. 21 n. 1). More technical aspects of 17th-century Dutch rigging are found in Asaert, *et al.*, *Maritieme Geschiedenis der Nederlanden*, II, *passim*.

[3] The *blinde* is a square sail raised under the bowsprit (Ratelband, *Reizen naar West-Afrika*, p. 21 n. 1).

rudder, steering with the fore-sail. Discovered the next day that we had sailed without rudder around twenty-five or twenty-six along the coast of Barberyen [= Barbary].

the 10th day. When the wind had abated a bit, we got the rudder in its place again, after repairing it as much as possible.

the 21st day. In the morning we were right beside the island of Teneriffa [= Tenerife]. It is said that this peak[1] can sometimes be seen in clear weather from the island of Madeira, which is forty *Duytsse* miles away.[2] It is amazing that this aforementioned peak lies so thick with snow despite the sun, which shines daily on it. We decided with the others to call in at Caep de Blanck [= Cap Blanc[3]] to see if we would find any fishermen.[4]

the 24 day. We arrived in the morning at Cabo de Blanck [= Cap Blanc]. Anchored at three fathoms. The cape lies at the latitude of 20 degrees 28 minutes.

Came to anchor leeward of Capo de Blanck [=Cap Blanc]

the 26th day. Now that we had caught scores of good-looking fish with our drag-nets, and saw no ships,[5] we sailed in the evening with our course set out of the shallows and for Cabo Verde. This aforementioned Caep de Blanck [= Cap Blanc] is tremendously arid and is just parched sand.[6] This place is full of many wild beasts, like lions,

[1] This peak is the summit of Pico de Teyde, which rises to 12,220 feet and was a common navigational landmark for mariners of this period.

[2] It is possible that here too, *Duytsse* meant 'Dutch' (see p. 36, n.1), but the composition of the sentence, 'It is said ...', certainly makes it possible that he consulted a source that measured the distance in German miles. Compare Van den Broecke's observation of the peak with that of Samuel Brun: 'so bey klarem Wätter auff die 40. Meilen weit gesehen wirdt' (Naber, *Samuel Brun's Schiffarten*, p. 3).

[3] The Portuguese maintained a fort (built in 1448) on Arguim, a small island 6 km off Cap Blanc, and traded there for gold dust, slaves, ostrich feathers, gum and salt (Davies, *A Primer of Dutch Seventeenth-Century Overseas Trade*, p. 33; Brooks, *Landlords and Strangers*, pp. 125–7).

[4] The *Neptunnis*'s state of disrepair forced the ship to limp down the coast, hoping to find another ship with parts to repair the rudder bracing.

[5] Still searching for a ship with a rudder bracing to spare; see previous note.

[6] In the early 17th century, Cap Blanc lay on the furthest northern margins of land suitable for agriculture (Webb, *Desert Frontier*, p. 7). Ruiters also described Cap Blanc as extremely arid (Naber, *Toortse der Zee-Vaert*, p. 47).

hart, tigers,[1] and camels. Around twenty to thirty Moors live there, very miserably. They must make do with only brackish water. Around here the Portuguese have a small fort [to protect them] from the Moors and wild animals. Around this fort much ambergris and elephant's tusks are available. The Portuguese come every year to this coast to fish, which brings them good profits in Portugal.[2]

Last day. We arrived leeward of Refusco [= Rufisque] at Capo Verde. Found a *doch boot*[3] here, with master Pieter Cornelissen Viel.[4] We dropped anchor and traded hides at a steady price, to wit, at the rate of one and half hides per bar [of iron].[5]

February [1608]

the 3rd day. A French sloop came there full of hides from Portodaele [= Portudal] on the account of the French captain named Barbau, who had sailed down the coast with a *travoado* in which five Frenchmen drowned. After which, he dragged up the sloop [that had sank] again, with 400 hides and 300 iron bars.

Came with the ship the *Neptunis* to Portodale [=Portudal]

the 5th day. Lifted our anchor and sailed to Portodaele [= Portudal], where we arrived in the evening. Found the ship the *Morinne* from Amsterdam on the roadstead there. The master was Theunis

[1] As tigers are an Asian, not African, feline, Van den Broecke's 'tigers' are probably another, African cat. European travellers commonly called leopards 'tigers' by mistake. Van den Broecke himself had already confused these two creatures and then self-corrected his error in his entry for 18 December 1605.

[2] These were indeed rich fishing waters, thanks to abundant plankton, and were frequented by Portuguese and Spanish ships (Brooks, *Landlords and Strangers*, pp. 125–6). See also Ruiters (Naber, *Toortse der Zee-Vaert*, pp. 47–8).

[3] The term d*och boot* (alternatively *dogboot* or *dogger*) designates a fishing-vessel of about eight lasts and with two square-rigged masts, one at mid-deck and one aft (Asaert, *et al.*, *Maritieme Geschiedenis der Nederlanden*, II, p. 49).

[4] The master Pieter Cornelissen Viel may have been the same person who formed a convoy with Van den Broecke on the author's first trip to Cape Verde. In the journal of his first voyage, Van den Broecke recorded the name of a master Pieter Cornelissen Uil, who was bound for the West Indies to get tobacco (see entry for 30 November 1605).

[5] Clearly an actual iron bar, and not the unit of 'bar' currency of the 18th and 19th centuries, which was an assortment of goods.

Jacoppsen from Memelick [= Medemblik[1]] who also had dropped anchor and traded.

the 6th day. In the morning we decided to go ashore but we met along the way with one Hans de Haese,[2] who must stay here for the term of three years as chief merchant at thirty guilders per month. I was already acquainted with him and had him as a guest on board. Towards evening, I went ashore with the same Hans de Haese and went to the house of a Portuguese named Symon Rodrigos, who had formerly been a most able merchant in Amsterdam.

the 7th day. We decided, despite not being able to get a pintle, to raise our anchor and to run to the coast of Guinea, which we did immediately. Made our course south-west out to sea. The wind here always blows north-east year in, year out.

the 25th day. In the morning we landed on the west coast of Cap de

[1] On the Zuiderzee (now, IJsselmeer) coast of Noord-Holland province. The Zuiderzee towns were among the first to send ships to Africa, principally to fetch salt from Atlantic islands with which they could barrel herring; French salt from La Rochelle was available to Dutch herring curers, but had too much magnesium to be suitable (Israel, *Dutch Primacy in World Trade*, pp. 137–8). After Barent Ericksz accidentally learned of Portuguese trade with West Africa and then made it back home to Medemblik, investors in this port city organized pioneering Dutch trade voyages to West Africa.

[2] De Haese (or De Haze) was probably of the emigrant Jewish Portuguese merchant diaspora in the northern Netherlands. See entry for 1 November 1609, in which Van den Broecke referred to him as 'this Portuguese' (and hinted that he had the same employer as himself). His surname may suggest this, as many old Jewish names in the Netherlands were taken from animals (here *haas*, meaning 'hare'). Friar Baltasar Barreira condemned the presence of Dutch traders on the Petite Côte and, in particular, that of a 'Dutch heretic' resident at Portudal, c.1606 (Brásio, *Monumenta missionaria africana*, sér. 2, IV, p. 382); perhaps De Haese was this 'heretic'. The East Indian parts of Van den Broecke's journal contain many mentions of De Haese (Coolhaas, *Pieter van den Broecke in Asië*, pp. 132, 160–62, 166, 167, 170–72), and De Haese was indeed very successful there: in 1611 he was in VOC employ, was named to the Council of the Indies, and was director of trade for the Moluccas; in 1613 he was appointed visitor-general; in 1616 he was director at Coromandel; he returned home in 1628, and was a VOC *bewindhebber* for the Zeeland chamber of the company (IJzerman, *Cornelis Buysero te Bantam*, pp. 197, 200).

Arrived on the Grain Coast where the natives swear by dropping water into their eyes three times

Pal [= Cape Palmas], at 4 degrees 15 minutes on the Grain Coast.[1] Six to eight canoes [came over] full of blacks and refreshments like *bannannis*,[2] very nice apples,[3] rice,[4] grain or malaguetta pepper,[5] and also ten to twelve elephant's tusks. We couldn't understand them, nor they us. They were very eager for old or new iron. They didn't trust us. We had to first scoop water out of the sea with our hands three times and let it drop into our eyes, which seemed to be their oath.[6] Many Frenchmen come here every year to trade and then go from here to the Caep de Loep [= Cape Lopez] and from there cross over to the West Indies.[7] The natives take very good care of their

[1] Dutch and French crews which encroached on Portuguese-controlled areas on the Grain Coast found themselves in grave danger. Lisbon repeatedly complained about foreign interlopers in 1607–8, and coastal sources boasted that they had massacred a Dutch crew and had attempted to seize a French ship (Brásio, *Monumenta missionaria africana*, sér. 2, IV, pp. 239–40).

[2] The identification of *bannanus* (with many spelling variations) here and in other early texts requires careful scrutiny by historians of African food systems. Many early visitors to this part of the African coast distinguished between the starchy plantains (often named *banannus* and *brodi*) and the fruity, sweet-tasting banana (often referred to as *bachoven*). For the history of plantains in Africa, see Rossel, *Taxonomic-Linguistic Study of Plantain in Africa*. This was perhaps Van den Broecke's first encounter with the fruits. See below, in his 'Report on Loango', where he may make such a distinction between the varieties.

[3] The 'apples' here are probably oranges (the modern Dutch word is *sinaasappel*, 'Chinese apple'), of either the sweet variety (*Citrus sinensis*) or the sour, 'Seville' type (*C. aurantium*).

[4] The rice mentioned here may be have been the Asian *Oryza sativa*, introduced by the Portuguese from Asia. For a discussion of pre-colonial agriculture just further east and the suggestion that the rice grown there might have been the indigenous *Oryza glaberrima*, see Claude Hélène Perrot, 'Semallies et moissons dans la région d'Assinie'.

[5] Malaguetta pepper *(Aframonum melegueta)*, also known as 'grains of Paradise', whence the name 'Grain Coast' applied by Europeans to the area where it was obtained, principally south of Cape Mount. See Müller's description for African methods of cultivating and producing malaguetta, as well as his thoughts on European preferences for East Indian peppers (Jones, *German Sources*, p. 229).

[6] This practice was noted by some of the earliest European visitors. See the observations of Towerson in the mid 16th-century (Blake, *Europeans in West Africa*, p. 376); also Ulsheimer (Jones, *German Sources*, p. 25, with n. 23) and Ruiters (Naber, *Toortse der Zee-Vaert*, p. 69).

[7] This sailing route was not exclusively French. Ships of all flags loaded African products such as pepper, ivory, slaves and gold on the western coast, then sailed to this Cape to take on victuals and firewood, and take the equatorial winds blowing to

praukens[1] in which no more than three men can sit. This place and its surroundings produce more than 100 lasts of malaguetta or grain annually, from which the coast takes its name. We anchored at fifteen fathoms, and about a cannon-shot away from land, on very loose anchorage. Here we have punctually a land wind in the morning and a sea wind in the afternoon.

March [1608]

the 2nd day. In the morning we were right beside the land of QuaQua,[2] [with] the Caep d'Appollonni [= Cape Apollonia] aside from us, rising up in two high hills. A *prauw* with three blacks came alongside us, calling out that here there was much *sica* (which gold is called here),[3] but then the scoundrels would not produce.[4]

---

the west. West India-bound ships would cross the Atlantic, while ships destined for European home ports would sail north from the mid-Atlantic.

[1] With the word *praukens,* Van den Broecke was probably trying to form a Dutch diminutive plural of Malay and Javanese words *perahow, prahoe,* and *praoe*, used for small canoes with outriggers and sometimes with small triangular sails. These words seeped into the language of Dutch mariners as *parahoe*, *parao*, or *prauw* (and became the rather obscure English word 'proa'). De Marees devoted an entire chapter to these canoes (Van Dantzig and Jones, *Pieter de Marees*, ch. 28). The canoes of the Grain Coast were often noticed to be smaller than elsewhere; see Ulsheimer (Jones, *German Sources*, p. 25) and Lübelfing (ibid., p. 11).

[2] This area, now eastern Côte d'Ivoire (Ivory Coast), was so named by Europeans in the 17th century because the Africans there greeted with the word 'Quaqua' (Van Dantzig and Jones, *Pieter de Marees*, p. 16, n. 9). See also Ruiters (*Toortse der Zee-Vaert*, p. 71) and Ulsheimer (Jones, *German Sources*, p. 20). For possible etymologies, see Jones, *German Sources*, pp. 20–21 n. 5.

[3] *Sika* was the word for 'gold' on the Gold Coast. The term originated among the Twi-speaking communities of the forested interior of the Gold Coast, who mined and panned for the precious metal, and was borrowed alongside trade in the metal by many of their West African neighbours.

[4] *Dan de fiellen wilden niet over commen.* The sense of this passage is that the African traders could not produce the gold which they reported was available or, colloquially, 'come through with the deal.' In fact, the reported availability of gold may have been no more than a lure, as De Marees reported that gold was rarely sold on the Grain Coast (Van Dantzig and Jones, *Pieter de Marees*, p. 14), as also did Brun (Jones, *German Sources*, p.64). Cf. however, Tilleman's observation that there was 'good gold to be had' there at the end of the 17th century (Winsnes, *Eric Tilleman*, p. 19).

the 3rd day. In the evening we were beside Cabo de tres Puntos [= Cape Three Points]. While sailing saw a small castle nearby named Huys te Sijnne [= Axim[1]] where around eighteen to twenty Portuguese live and trade much gold with the natives.

Came for the first time at the roadstead of Cammende [=Komenda] on the Gold Coast

the 4th day. We arrived in the morning at Cammende [= Komenda] on the Gold Coast. We found here a ship from Doort [= Dordrecht] with chief factor Carel van der Goes, brother of the general[2] Adriaen van der Goes.[3] He provided us with two very good rudder pintles. I went ashore immediately with a *prau* to buy provisions for the ship and came shortly after midday on board again. Raised our anchor in the evening, and went along the shore so close to the castle De Mijnne [= Elmina] that they could easily have fired upon us. In the evening near sundown we came to Cabo Corsse [= Cape Coast], which lies about five miles from Cammende [= Komenda], where the castle De Miner [= Elmina] lies in the middle. We anchored at five fathoms beside the ship named the *Morinne*, on which was the general Adriaen van der Goes. Here lay three other ships and at least four sloops, from which all the masters and most of the merchants came aboard. This place of Cabo Cors [= Cape Coast] is now one of the principal trading places on the entire coast. Those ships have an agreement, giving sixty sticks[4] of linen for a *bende*[5] gold. Each stick

[1] The Portuguese fort there was named 'Atsijn' on Hans Prophet's 1629 map of the Gold Coast.

[2] A 'general' was a commander in charge of the lead-ship in a group of three or more ships (Ratelband, *Reizen naar West-Afrika*, p. 24 n. 8).

[3] Adriaen van der Goes had been made 'general' by ships including Ulsheimer's (Jones, *German Sources*, pp. 23, 26). Van der Goes (of Rotterdam, died 1649) was married to Regina de Marez (died 1624), Pieter de Marees's aunt (Ratelband, *Reizen naar West-Afrika*, p. lxiv).

[4] 'Sticks' were a measure of length for cloth. As Ulsheimer observed: 'Linen is measured out with a staff or stick, about as long as 1½ of our ells' (Jones, *German Sources*, p. 34). De Marees calculated that 1¾ sticks equaled 2 fathoms, c. 1601 (Van Dantzig and Jones, *Pieter de Marees*, p. 61).

[5] The origin of the term *benda* is uncertain. Gerrard conjectured that it might be derived from the Portuguese words 'banda' or 'barra', denoting a flat metal bar. The weight of a *benda* varied with time and place (eg. De Marees noted that the *benda* of Accra was lighter than that of Mouri), but in general was about two Troy ounces, or about 61 grams (Garrard, *Akan Weights and the Gold Trade*, pp. 250–53).

was one and a half Dutch ells,[1] and the *bende* is two ounces, worth sixty-two Dutch guilders.[2]

the 10th day. After I had been ashore, we sailed to Cap de Loop [= Cape Lopez] in the company of Claes Jorissen, master from Rotterdam, who was destined homeward.

Arrived at Cabo Coors [=Cape Coast] and left again from there for Cabo de Lop [=Cape Lopez]

the 21st day. We sighted the island Isla de Prince [= Príncipe] east-north-east from us and the island Ste. Thome [= São Tomé] behind us.

the 25th day. In the morning we arrived leeward of the Capbo de Loep Gonsalvis [= Cape Lopez] and anchored offshore at twenty fathoms about a cannon-shot from shore. A large canoe with twenty-eight men came aboard. After midday the factor Harman Bitter sent me ashore. I was brought immediately to the chief who lived in a straw hut and had more than twenty women sitting around him. There he presented me immediately with one of them, and presented us with a pot of palm wine and a large bunch of *bannannes* [= plantains], which I immediately took with me back aboard.[3]

the 29th day. I traded cotton linen[4] for a batch of elephant's tusks. These tusks come mostly from Olibate,[5] where the king resides. The city lies a distance away, upriver. This aforementioned king wages war against those of the rivers d'Angre [= Corisco Bay] and Gabon

[1] A unit for measuring cloth. The length of ells varied widely, from the Flemish ell of 27 inches to the English ell of 45 inches.

[2] Cf. Ulsheimer's rate of 40 to 43 sticks of cloth per *benda* (Jones, *German Sources*, p. 34)

[3] See the anonymous Dutch manuscript of c.1642–55 edited by Adam Jones (*West Africa in the Seventeenth Century*, p. 35): 'Although you may hope to pay nothing here, they are great spongers. The Priest (*Paep*), whom they regard almost as if he were their king, will bring you a pot of mead wine and a bunch of bananas; but he wants to have them paid for with return gifts. You give him only enough to get rid of him, in order to preserve your honour.' For other descriptions of conducting trade here, see Brun (Jones, *German Sources*, pp. 70–71), and Ruiters (Naber, *Toortse der Zee-Vaert*, pp. 85–7).

[4] A linen-like fabric made from cotton, rather than European flax, and which was probably an import from Asia.

[5] Alternatively 'Olibatta', a village on the Nazareth mouth of the Ogooué River. Patterson suggested that this name was probably derived from the Kikongo *libata,* meaning 'town' (Patterson, *The Northern Gabon Coast to 1875*, p. 20).On the town, see also De Marees (Van Dantzig and Jones, *Pieter de Marees*, p. 241) and Brun (Jones, *German Sources*, p. 71).

[= the Gabon estuary], both of which are very beautiful rivers.[1] It is terribly unhealthy here. Those who travel upriver from Oli Batten will usually fall sick. One cannot keep the women here off of oneself or away from the lodge, so lecherous are the people you find here.[2] On this same day I caught so many fish with one draw of the net, that the crews of the two ships could be fed with them. Was also there when one draw of the net produced 2,808 mullet and other kinds of delicious fish.[3]

April [1608]

the 3rd day. Once we were supplied with water and firewood, [we] raised our anchor in the morning and went to sea.

the 4th day. We sailed again towards land. On coming there, we found that we were a mile leeward of the cape [= Cape Lopez] and had drifted a bit towards the bay.[4]

the 5th day. In the morning we came again for the second time to the cape [= Cape Lopez].

the 7th day. Sailed again with a south-south-east wind.

[1] On relations between the communities, see the description by 'D.R.' (probably Dierick Ruiters) in De Marees (Van Dantzig and Jones, *Pieter de Marees*, pp. 234–7). Van Wassenaer recorded the same hostilities towards communities to the north (*Historisch verhael*, October 1624: f. 29v).

[2] *Man can de vrouwen met gewelt van lijf oft longie niet houden, sulscken lucsiriuis volck hebt ghij hierr*. The word *lucsiriuis* (modern Dutch, *luxurieus*) is a form of the old French word *lecherie*, 'lechery', and is similar to the word *luxurie*, which fellow-émigré Pieter de Marees used to describe African women who ate too many bananas, a supposed aphrodisiac (Van Dantzig and Jones, *Pieter de Marees*, p. 162, with n. 5). Could it have been slang from Antwerp? Many European visitors at this time described the local women as debauched; see Jones, *German Sources*, p. 72 n.172.

[3] Van den Broecke's precision in the number of small fish caught is curious, indeed, and may merely have been a slip of the pen. The editions published in 1634 printed the number at '2800'.

[4] Van den Broecke repeated this course to western Central Africa on each subsequent voyage. His ships would sail eastward along the coast of West Africa and then veer south-east near São Tomé, where they hoped to catch storm winds to blow them through the doldrums near the equator and further south, against the northward Benguela current (see Van den Broecke's summary of this strategy in the 'Report on the Kingdom of Loango' attached to the his journal, below pp. 93–4).

the 10th day. The wind was west-north-west, [and made our] course to the south. Our colleague, Claes Jorissen, took leave of us this night to return to the Fatherland.

the 11th day. The wind and course were as before. At midday we measured[1] [our ship to be] at 2 degrees 20 minutes south of the equator. On this day we caught a dorado[2] five feet long, which had in its throat a flying fish one and a quarter feet long.

the 16th and 17th days. Wind and course were as before, namely [the wind was] north and our course was south by east. At noon we measured 4 degrees 20 minutes latitude.

the 21st day. Had wind off the land in the morning. We were at the latitude of 4 degrees and 56 minutes. Turned again toward sea with the aforementioned land wind, and then in the afternoon turned again with the sea wind toward land, where we stopped and dropped anchor.

the 22nd day. At midday, with a zenith measurement of 5 degrees 6 minutes, we raised our anchor and went with the wind along the coast. Came into Conno bay [= Pointe Noire] which we thought was Loango.[3] Saw fifty to sixty canoes going past our ship, which surprised us, and we figured therefore that it must not be Loango. Went again out of this bay and came three miles north at last in the bay of Loango. On coming there, we found our other ship here lying here at the roadstead, with master Jan Janssen Backer and chief factor Wemmer van Barchum, who sat in chains because of his great arrogance.[4]

Came for the first time with the ship the *Neptunis* in the bay of Loango

[1] That is, with a sextant or an astrolabe.

[2] *Dorradis* (*Coryphaena hippurus*) from the Portuguese *dourada*, 'golden, gilt', and also the name given to the fish in that language. In English it is known, in addition to dorado, as gold mackerel. See also De Marees's description (Van Dantzig and Jones, *Pieter de Marees*, p.154)

[3] Their ship had gone too far south.

[4] Wemmer van Berchum's personality spoiled many of his professional relationships. To warrant imprisonment on the *Merman*, he had probably transgressed the authority of the ship's master during the battle described below. Van Berchum (1585–1653) was from a wealthy Gelderland family. He later served as VOC director on the Coromandel Coast in 1612–15. In that role he attracted similar complaints about his demeanour. An alternative version of how the battle on the Congo unfolded – which credited the Dutch victory to his heroic leadership, and had him personally honoured by the 'Kongo King' – appeared in print

This place is easily recognized because at 5 degrees [latitude] there is no higher land than this place until at Cascais,[1] which lies at 6 degrees. These hills are very easy to recognize because the earth is red. On the south side of the entrance to this aforementioned bay, you must beware of a bank or reef, which runs out to sea a half mile south-west of the southern cape and is a foot less than three fathoms deep. [And beware that] after passing that you sail so close to land that you could recognise someone, because about a musket-shot from land is clay bottom, at just three fathoms. Once we came to a rest, the junior factor from the other ship, named Pieter Tiellemanssen, came aboard and he told us how they had battled against four Portuguese ships in the river Congo, one of which they had shot and sunk, and the three others they had chased away. Also [heard] that the yacht the *Mermine*, now with Pieter Brandt, lay and traded in [the] Congo.

Heard that the Portuguese here at Loango had shot dead with a flintlock the master of the same yacht, named Augustijn Cornelissen, thinking that he was Pieter Brandt, whom they loathed unto death because he had revealed this place to our company.[2] The Portuguese invited Pieter Tillemans, Pieter Brandt and the master to

on the eve of his nomination to the vice-admiralty of Holland and West Friesland in 1627 (Van Wassenaer, *Historisch verhael*, June 1627: ff. 25–28v; Ratelband, *Reizen naar West-Afrika*, pp. lxxxix–xc; Bruijn, *The Dutch Navy of the Seventeenth and Eighteenth Centuries*, p. 48).

[1] Cascais, a harbour on the south side of the Chiloango river, was the principal Atlantic outlet of the African state of Kakongo.

[2] Unfortunately, Van den Broecke did not elaborate on the membership of this company. Gerard Reynst and Lucas van der Venne were mentioned by the States-General on 6 August 1610, as the first to navigate and trade at Congo, Loango, and Angola (Van Deursen, *Resolutiën der Staten-Generaal, Part 1*, p. 196; see also p. 189 for Reynst and Company's involvement in Guinea trade). If this company was indeed the first, then it must relate to more than a decade earlier; Van Noort recorded news of Dutch ships trading in 'the Congo' (that is, presumably the river mouth) in late 1598, when he visited Cape Lopez. Upon Van Noort's return to the Netherlands, he invested in 1601 in the outfitting of a trade ship bound for Angola and Brazil, with one Pieter Brandt of Ilpendam as factor (see IJzerman, *De Reis om de Wereld door Oliver van Noort*, pp. 43, 45 n. 2, 52 n. 3, 94). Pieter Brandt may have enjoyed an unusually long career in Central Africa; as late as 1620, a report to the Spanish king complained of a Dutch trader named 'Pero Abrantes' who traded regularly in the Congo area (Ratelband, *Reizen naar West-Afrika*, pp. lxxxviii–lxxxix).

visit them. But Pieter Brandt, who was ill, or because his heart gave him warning, excused himself for that time and let the other two aforenamed persons[1] go. And because the master had no hat to wear, he borrowed Pieter Brandt's. The Portuguese saw him coming and thought that he was Pieter Brandt. As the *schuijdt*[2] came alongside the ship they shot him dead with a long flintlock, and then the others were immediately taken prisoner to be taken to Loando de St. Pauwel [= Luanda; São Paulo de Luanda]. This they would have accomplished if the king of Loango's people had not followed them. [They] took them from Portuguese and right then and there struck the Portuguese master dead with elephant's tusks. Well, the Portuguese were forced to pay a large fine, which clearly showed that the natives were loyal to our nation.

Here we also learned that the little ship from Doordt [= Dordrecht] was taken by betrayal at the island of Ste Thome [= São Tomé] and was taken by surprise. From there it was immediately sent to Portugal with its crew and cargo.[3]

the 23rd day. It was decided that the Governor-General[4] Wemmer van Barchum was to be released from his shackles, and that no more would be said about the aggravation he had caused.[5] Furthermore it was decided that the ship the *Merman* would be the first to travel south to Congo to trade elephant's tusks.

May [1608]

First day. Traded for the first time fourteen pieces of elephant's tusks, which weighed 200 lb, at 3,000 *réis* for the *quintal* of 120 Dutch lb. Here I paid with eleven ells of red *vierlooden*[6] worth

[1] That is, junior factor Pieter Tiellemanssen and master Augustijn Cornelissen.

[2] A small boat or launch used to manoeuvre where the large ship could not, such as in shallow water, rivers, and in this case, to move men between two large ships.

[3] Van den Broecke had just visited this 'ship from Doort': see entry for 4 March 1608.

[4] This must be a mistake for 'general'.

[5] Indeed, Van den Broecke himself made no mention of this incident in the published accounts of his travels; see the Introduction, pp. 13–14, 14 n. 1.

[6] *Vierlooden* was a heavy red cloth with four lead seals indicating its high quality.

Went ashore at Loango for the first time

twenty-two stuivers per ell.[1] On the same day I went ashore for the first time at Loango and was invited by the king, who gave me twenty cloths[2] so that I could buy palm wine for them.[3] Returned aboard in the evening.

the 27th day. The chief factor sent me with a present for the king, [and] to request a license for our yacht to go from here to Mayomber [= Mayoumba], which is under the rule of the king. He granted us that and lent us four of his nobles for that purpose.

June [1608]

the 11th day. In the early morning we saw four sea-horses[4] on the

[1] These tusks which Van den Broecke bought were small and second-rate, averaging 14.3 Dutch lb (= 4.29 kg.; or at the ratio of 1 Dutch *pond* to 1.1 English pounds = 15.71 English pounds). On his voyage to Cape Verde, Van den Broecke paid 15 to 16 bars of iron for a *quintal* of large, first-rate tusks which averaged 50 *ponden* in weight. Feinberg calculated even lighter averages for first-rate tusks bought by Dutch traders in the 18th century (see Feinberg and Johnson, 'The West African Ivory Trade during the Eighteenth Century', pp. 441, 452–3).

[2] Palms were a source of weaving material indigenous to the moister areas of western Central Africa. Men stripped fibres from their fronds and wove them into square cloths called *libongos* (Martin, 'Power, Cloth, and Currency on the Loango Coast', p. 41; Hilton, *The Kingdom of Kongo*, p. 6; Miller, *Way of Death*, p. 54).

[3] Palm-wine drinkers in the drier parts of southern Loango eagerly awaited shipments of this alcoholic drink from the better-watered northern coast, where the tapping season began earlier; for example, Van den Broecke found palm wine available at Cape Lopez in his entry for 25 March 1608, and Brun commented on seasonal shortages in Loango (Jones, *German Sources*, p. 54). Dutch traders like Van den Broecke made their initial entry into African trade by hauling locally-made trade items (here in western Central Africa they carried, palm wine, cloth, and takula) which were in regional demand.

[4] Van den Broecke wrote *Zee parden* (lit. 'sea-horses'), which is modern Dutch for walruses, but these are not found in tropical Africa. He may have merely been translating directly into Dutch the Portuguese term *calvo do mar* (lit. 'sea horse'), which denotes hippopotamuses. The illustrator for the 1634 Haarlem edition of Van den Broecke's book certainly thought that they were hippopotamuses – he drew several emerging from the ocean alongside a beached giant squid. These hippopotamuses are depicted with odd, curved tusks, perhaps to match the printed text of that volume, which also likened the tusks to those of a wild boar. It is possible, however, that Van den Broecke never saw a hippopotamus in Loango; he never indicated that he travelled far enough inland to see these creatures, which are in fact restricted to non-tidal, inland streams. His manuscript, as well as the text of

beach which were about to graze on the green fields. I went immediately by boat to look at them. As I came near them, they remained looking at us for so long that, because we had no weapons, we did not dare go closer. Then they went step by step towards the water and then dove under.

They appear as follows: big and thick as a buffalo but somewhat heavier of body; short legs; cleft feet like a clover leaf; short little tails; ears like a *moets* horse;[1] broad mouth with two large round striking-tusks like a wild boar. They snort like the horses in our country.

The figure of a sea-horse.

[blank space in the manuscript]

August [1608]

the 8th day. In the morning I sailed with the yacht the *Merminne* to the river Congo. I arrived, after many difficulties, only on the 24th at

the published editions and the illustration presented there, have these creatures implausibly walking out of the sea onto the beach. If he had never in fact seen these creatures, he would have based his description on what he had heard while in Africa (perhaps in the Portuguese language, which he translated into Dutch), or what he read upon returning to Europe. For example, Battel described hippopotamuses, in English, as 'sea horses' (Ravenstein, *Strange Adventures*, p. 64), as also did De Marees (Van Dantzig and Jones, *Pieter de Marees*, pp. 11, 242). An alternative possibility is that Van den Broecke merely muddled the name for what he saw, if he did indeed see a hippopotamus; the Dutch word most commonly used in early texts (and it is also the modern Dutch word) to describe hippopotamuses is *nijlpaarden* ('Nile horses'), while the Dutch word *zeekoeien* ('sea-cows') indicates manatees. Samuel Brun similarly confused 'sea-horses' and 'sea-cows' in German (Jones, *German Sources*, pp. 59–60). Alternatively again (but least likely), Van den Broecke may have been combining ideas about the 'horse-sea monster' of Greek and Roman mythology (*hippocampus*), perhaps still current then among mariners.

[1] Meaning unclear; presumably this was a domestic creature with which Dutch readers would be familiar. Ratelband suggested *muilpaard* (roughly, 'mule-horse'), an old and somewhat unusual form of the Dutch *muildier*, 'mule' (Ratelband, *Reizen naar West-Afrika*, p. 30 n. 3). But a mule's characteristically large ears have little in common with the small ears of a hippopotamus. The text of the published editions do little to help identify what Van den Broecke meant in comparing this creature to a *moetspardt*, as these altered this passage to compare this African animal's head, rather than its ears, to that of this other Dutch domestic creature, stating that they had 'heads like *moedts-peerden* with short ears' (*hebben hoofden als moedts-peerden met corte ooren*): Van den Broecke, *Korte Historiael* (Haarlem edition), f. 12v.

the ship the *Merman* of Jan Janssen Backer and chief factor Wemmer van Barchum.

September [1608]

the first day. The general Wemmer van Barchum sent me with Baltasaer Jacodt, his clerk, to the town of Schonho [= Sonyo], [and there] to the count with a letter of credentials to request permission from him [to trade]. This count keeps his residence in a town named Bansa de Schonno [= Mbanza Sonyo], around seven miles upriver.[1] When I came to him, he sat on a Spanish chair with a red velvet covering and covered with gold tacks. This stool stood on an expensive *alcatiffa*.[2] His clothing was a red damask robe with three wide gold trimmings, a black embroidered hat[3] with gold and pearls, which his subjects had themselves made. On his neck hung a thick gold chain, wrapped three times around his neck. His subjects respect him greatly. The principal nobles stood by him with precious robes and hats in their hands. He knows how to maintain his authority despite the fact that he is blind. They said that he was over 140 years old.[4] His son read him the letter, which was written in Portuguese, in perfect form.[5] This count is named Dom Migiel, count of Sonho

[1] Mbanza Sonyo lay on a creek about 25 km from the river's mouth (see Jones, *German Sources*, pp. 58–9, n. 85).

[2] A Portuguese word for 'carpet', derived from the Arabic *al-katifah*.

[3] Special caps called *mpu* were significant insignia of political and religious authority in the kingdom of Kongo at this time (Hilton, *Kingdom of Kongo*, pp. 37, 40, 96, 118, 138, 157; Gibson and McGurk, 'High-Status Caps of the Kongo and Mbundu Peoples').

[4] Ratelband made the unlikely suggestion that the Africans counted two years to every European calendar year, thus making the king only 70 years old (Ratelband, *Reizen naar West-Afrika*, p. xci). Could it be, however, that the reported age of the *mani* Sonyo referred not to his individual age, but instead to the antiquity of the members of the Da Silva group holding that position, thus supplying additional evidence that the Silvas were positioned in Sonyo before Miguel's accession in the late 16th century (see Hilton, *Kingdom of Kongo*, p. 124)? Note that the 1634 published editions changed the age from 140 to 110 years (Haarlem edition, p. 14). Brun reported that this ruler was 150 years old (Jones, *German Sources*, p. 62).

[5] Literacy was held in high esteem, and provincial governors often sent their male children away to missionary-run schools. Most of these schools were in Mbanza Kongo (São Salvador), though some of the richer provincial capitals did

[= Sonyo].[1] He keeps very good law and order in his land. They are mostly Christians[2] and go to mass every day, twice a day when it rains. They maintain five or six churches and have a Portuguese priest named Dom Gonsalvis who teaches them everything. There are eight to ten schools here like those in Portugal, where all the children are instructed and taught in Portuguese. Everyone goes the whole day with a book in hand and with a rosary. They are a very friendly people, of sturdy body, and courageous in battle. They handle weapons exceptionally well, and they are moreover clever in all of their business. The women do most of the work, like ploughing the land,[3] seeding, and weeding, so that they provide sufficiently for their husband.

The count adheres to a custom, which is very old, that if there is a pretty young maiden then he sleeps with her, and as soon as she is with child he gives her with her child to [one of] his most principal nobles, who are therefore very favoured, for he usually gives many goods with her.[4]

---

support schools for children of the *Mwissikingo* elite (Hilton, *Kingdom of Kongo*, p. 79).

[1] 'Migiel, Count of Sonho,' is certainly Miguel da Silva, *mani* Sonyo ('lord or governor of Sonyo'). Miguel was (perhaps) the first of the powerful Kongo aristocratic alliance of Da Silva to be appointed governor of Sonyo, some time in the late 16th century. In the first decade of the 17th century, he sought independence from the Kongo kingdom and rebelled against *mani* Kongo Alvaro II, killing several of his nobles in the process (Hilton, *Kingdom of Kongo*, pp. 124–5). Brun recorded the *mani* Sonyo's name as 'Don Ferdinado' (Jones, *German Sources*, p. 62).

[2] By the time of Van den Broecke's visit, the Christian community of Kongo was already over 100 years old. The first convert was the king of Kongo, Nzinga a Nkuwu, who was baptized (as João I) in 1491. The early history of the Kongolese Catholic church is described in Thornton, 'The Development of an African Catholic Church in the Kingdom of Kongo'.

[3] Although Van den Broecke uses the verb *ploegen*, African farmers in fact worked the land with hoes, in the absence of ploughs.

[4] Beyond Van den Broecke's view were contentious lineage politics. In the analysis of Anne Hilton, women and children were the medium of exchange between two separate and competing bases of power: that of the local, matrilineal descent groups (*kanda*) and patrilineal categories of *Mwissikongo* elite from which the *mani* Sonyo was centrally-appointed. The child produced by this union of *mani* Sonyo and local concubine would belong to both the father's patrilineal category and the mother's *kanda*. The 'principal nobles' whom the *mani* Sonyo favoured with these exchanges were other *Mwissikongo* (Hilton, *Kingdom of Kongo*, pp. 124–5).

He lodged me in the house of one of the chief men, to which abundant food was sent from the court each morning and evening. The head of our house was named Dom Simon Seloti, who also showed us great friendship and courtesy.

the 4th day. In the morning I took my leave from the count, who gave me a hammock in which I was carried to the river where our boat lay waiting.[1] Along the way we saw large numbers of stock, for example wild animals such as hart, hind,[2] field-fowl,[3] wild pigs,[4] and others too; and, particularly, many oxen, cows, sheep, and goats, which were pastured in flocks of 100 by the herdsmen. We passed by many pretty villages. These sheep have short hair and have long manes, like the horses in our country.[5]

The figure of a sheep in Congo.

[blank space in the manuscript]

the 6th day. I went again to see the count of Sonho [= Sonyo] with Wemmer van Barchum, where we were well received.

Sailed out of Congo with the yacht the *Merminne* to go to Loango

the 11th day. I went with the yacht the *Merminne* out of the Congo River to Loango, where on the 12th day I arrived at our ship the *Neptunus*, thanks to God.

the 20th day. After we had supplied the aforementioned yacht with a

[1] Hammocks had been introduced by the Portuguese early in the 16th century. These covered litters carried by two or four slaves were the general mode of transportation for European traders and African men of wealth until the 20th century (Hilton, *Kingdom of Kongo*, p. 84; Miller, *Way of Death*, pp. 191–2).

[2] A doe (i.e. female) of the same type of deer as the (male, or 'stag') hart.

[3] This was probably a species of pigeon, but perhaps was the indigenous African guinea-fowl (*Numida meleagris*). The first section of this sentence describes wild animals, so it is unlikely that Van den Broecke meant free-roaming domestic fowl (*Gallus gallus*). For fowl in this area, see Vansina, *Paths in the Rainforests*, p. 290 n. 77.

[4] These 'wild pigs' were probably warthogs (*Phacochoerus aethiopicus*); see Vansina, *Paths in the Rainforests*, p. 290 n. 78.

[5] The thin-tailed hair sheep (*Ovis aries*) is well adapted to high-rainfall tropical forests; see Blench, 'Prehistory of African Ruminant Livestock'. But such great numbers of grass-feeding stock were unusual in forest-savanna mosaic areas like Sonyo (see Vansina, *Paths in the Rainforests*, p. 92).

cargo of 12,000 guilders [in trade goods] from both of the ship's cargoes, I left with Pieter Tillemans for the Gold Coast. May the Lord give us a safe journey, amen.

Went from Loango to the Gold Coast with the same ship

When I left, the ship the *Neptunis* in Loango had traded 1,788 pieces of elephant's tusks, weighing 37,213 Dutch lb. The cost of a *quintal* of 120 lb came to 3,211 *réis* with expenses and all. That equals seven and three quarter ells of *vierloodt* for the 120 lb, at the rate of one guilder per ell, so that 120 lb of tusks cost only 7: 12:8.[1]

the 27th day. In the morning we saw the island of Anna Bon [= Annobón] ahead to leeward.

October [1608]

the 6th day. We arrived at Commende [= Komenda] on the Grain Coast [sic: = Gold Coast]. Found three merchant ships already here, anchored and trading, namely the *Jonghen Tobias* with master Jan Jochumssen from Amsterdam and Chief Factor Jan Pieterssen Schoo. There was also the yacht of the man-eater Jan Cornelissen May,[2] and the master was Heyn Classen. There was a bark from Delft with master Jan Matheussen from Bollonnen [= Boulogne] and factor Willem den Dorst and junior factor Jacop Seggersen, son of the old general who perished at the Mijna [= Elmina] castle.[3] We understood immediately that they were bidding against each other and gave seventy to eighty sticks per *benda*. Stayed here to trade.

November [1608]

the 15th day. We sold our *jachtien*[4] to an English yacht belonging to

[1] This is an old accounting format, with colons separating columns for guilders, stuivers, and penningen. See p. 23 n. 1.

[2] The nickname 'man-eater' for Jan Cornelissen May was probably drawn from his last name, which is similar to the Dutch *made*, meaning 'maggot' (Ratelband, *Reizen naar West-Afrika*, p. 33 n. 3)

[3] Seggersen may have been a casualty of Carel Hulsher's (or Corolus Holscher) attack on Elmina castle in 1596 (Ratelband, *Reizen naar West-Afrika*, p. 33 n. 6; Van Dantzig and Jones, *Pieter de Marees*, pp. 108–9).

[4] Like the *schuijdt* above, this was a small vessel useful in shallow coastal waters, rivers and lagoons.

captain Roudolf Cruw from London, for 2 lb of gold, in exchange for an English yacht.[1]

Came to anchor at Moure [=Mouri] and trade there

the 29th day. We raised our anchor and assumed we were sailing to Capo Cors [= Cape Coast], which we passed in the dark of night, and dropped anchor at Morre [= Mouri].[2] In the morning we saw that there were ships lying near us, and that one was named the *Hoep*, with factor Carrel Vergoes.[3] And there was the yacht the *Duyve*, with factor Lambert Janssen van der Mayden. The other was just a sloop, with junior factor Louwerens Cornelissen. On this same day, I traded for 1½ lb of gold. Morre [= Mouri] is at the latitude of 5 degrees north of the equator.

December [1608]

the 16th day. I was ashore by a river where the blacks caught a very large water snake thirteen and a half feet long and six palms thick.[4]

[blank space in the manuscript]

[1] The presence of an English vessel on the Gold Coast at this time is surprising. Although some English ships had visited the Gold Coast in the mid 16th-century, the English are usually thought not to have returned to trade here again until the 1630s (see Hair and Law, 'The English in Western Africa', p. 250). This English vessel appears to have been optimistic about conducting a substantial trade here – as they traded gold (which they had presumably acquired there, on the Gold Coast) in order to expand their capacity, and, it must be assumed, had enough trade-goods still in stock to justify a larger presence

[2] Mouri was a fishing village where the Dutch held their strongest commercial position for obtaining gold from the Elmina hinterland. Throughout the 1590s, various Dutch interlopers had tried to dislodge the Portuguese from Elmina, attacking by both land and sea, but to no avail. At the turn of the century Dutch ships began to call at the village of Mouri, just to the east of Elmina, to trade for gold. Mouri lay within territory of Asebu, which was at odds with its neighbour Fetu, to which Elmina belonged (Van Dantzig and Jones, *Pieter de Marees*, p. 8, with n. 8; Vogt, *Portuguese Rule on the Gold Coast*, ch. 6).

[3] Van den Broecke had met with chief factor Carel van der Goes (in this entry, 'Carel Vergoes') on the Gold Coast earlier, when the latter was aboard the little ship from Doordt. Later, Van den Broecke heard that this ship had been tricked into capture. See entries for 4 March 1608 and 22 April 1608.

[4] Compare this description with the large water snakes encountered by De Marees (Van Dantzig and Jones, *Pieter de Marees*, p. 128) and Hemmersam (Jones, *German Sources*, p. 126).

the 16th day. A sloop with factor Abraham Stoffelssen came there [= to Mouri] from Accara [= Accra] with a tailwind. This had never happened, as far as the Dutch and the natives could remember, that the current came out of the bight for seven days.[1]

For seven days the wind and current came out of the bight, which was surprising

January 1609 in Moure

the 7th day. Our ship the *Neptunis* arrived from Loango at Cabo Cours [= Cape Coast]. I went immediately to it aboard a herring-*schuydt* [= lighter].

the 10th day. I went again from the yacht the *Mermine* onto the *Neptunis,* because the blacks would have nothing to do with our chief factor Harman Bitter.

the 28th day. We raised our anchor and sailed to the roadstead at Morre [= Mouri] and made a convoy there with two other ships who wanted to return home with us. They were, namely, the boat of Jan Pieterssen with master Gerret Pietersen as admiral; and the *Jonghen Tobias*, with master Jan Jochumssen third in command; and our ship the *Neptunis* as vice-admiral.

the 30th day. Raised our anchor in the morning and went to Accra with a tailwind, to go from there to Cabo de Loep [= Cape Lopez].

the last day. We anchored at Barcou [= Beraku].[2] This place is very easy to recognise by the trees standing on the heights. Also, there lie great stone cliffs on the beach. Ships lie here at six fathoms. Three *prauws* with people and refreshments came aboard with many *patates*[3] and a little gold. In the evening raised our anchor and went to Jaccara [= Jakarta], I mean, Accara [= Accra].

February [1609]

The first day of February. Arrived in the morning at the Accara [= Accra] roadstead where there were twelve ships trading, to wit,

[1] The current typically runs eastward, towards the Bight of Benin. See, for example, De Marees's description (Van Dantzig and Jones, *Pieter de Marees*, pp. 85–6).

[2] Beraku is around 18 miles by sea west of Accra.

[3] This fruit often appears in early Dutch texts as *batate*, from the Portuguese *batata*, 'potato'. Here, it is probably a sweet potato (*Ipomoea batata*).

Came to Accara [=Accra]

the *Buys* from Delft with master Persse Pier or [= also known as] Pieter Cornelissen; and also the ship of Claes Heyn[1] with factor Romboudt Pijls; and the yacht of Hans Sabouts with factor Michiel Heynssen; and the *Duyfken* with factor Gerret Adrianssen; and the boat named *Morinne* with factor Cornelis Janssen. [There was] also a small boat, on which the factor was Isack Staes. In the evening we were all guests on the ship of our admiral Gerret Pieterssen and factor Harman de Laer, who gave us his farewell dinner.

The coast of Guinea gave in my time no more 1,800 lb. of gold

Out of the place of Accara [= Accra] comes the most and best gold of this whole coast, but the people here are very bad and evil people. It is very dangerous to come ashore here because of the large breakers. The entire coast gives annually 1,800 lb of gold, sometimes more, sometimes also slightly less.[2]

the 3rd day. In the morning before sunrise we set out under sail with a course for the Cabo de Loep Gonsalvis [= Cape Lopez]. On this day we weighed our gold in double leather sacks, 10 lb of gold in each sack. Found that there was 44 lb 2 oz, most of which I had personally traded, except for eight pounds by Pieter Tillemans.

the 17th day. We arrived at the Caebo de Loop Gonsalvis [= Cape Lopez].

We three left Cabo de Loep [=Cape Lopez] for the Fatherland

the 26th day. After we had traded our remaining cargo with the blacks for around forty-two *quintals* of tusks, and had provisioned ourselves with water and firewood for the homeward voyage, we sailed together for the Fatherland in the Name of God.

the 28th day. We found that we were [only] three miles out of the bight because of the strong current.

March [1609]

the 2nd day. In the morning we came again on the roadstead near the same Caebo de Loop [= Cape Lopez].

[1] Hendrick Ottsen met a 'Claes Heyn' while trading on the Gold Coast in January 1599 (IJzerman, *Journal van de Reis naar Zuid-Amerika door Hendrick Ottsen*, p. 8).

[2] Ulsheimer estimated that 1,500 to 1,600 lbs of gold were exported annually (Jones, *German Sources*, p. 26). For a discussion of the changing volume of West African gold exports, see Curtin, 'Africa in the Wider Monetary World'.

the 5th day. Left again together.

the 16th day. We caught more than 200 dorados but the other ships could not catch any. As darkness fell we caught a dorado five and a quarter feet long which had in its throat a flying-fish that was one and quarter feet long and had only just died.[1]

[blank space in the manuscript]

the 19th day. We saw a horned-fish[2] swimming behind our ship, which appeared to be over five fathoms long and its horn was a half of a fathom. The fins were blue and the body was light blue. So long as it kept around our ship, we saw no other fish. As they stayed put under the keel of the ship, we assumed that a fish like this one had rammed its horn with such force into this ship on its previous voyage, that it penetrated the pine wood and the oak wood and after that had gone at least three fingers deep into the timbers. This was only discovered in Amsterdam, when an extra skin was put onto the ship. The horn can now be seen in Amsterdam at the house of Bart Janssen Steenhuyssen.[3]

A horned-fish.

[blank space in the manuscript]

the 26th day. At midday we measured a latitude of 28 minutes south of the equator.

[1] This passage is nearly identical to the entry for 11 April 1608.

[2] Van den Broecke's description of the fish fits various species of the sawfish genus *Pristis*, which have horn-like snouts and are greyish in colour.

[3] Steenhuyssen (elsewhere recorded as Barthold Jansz Steenhuizen) was an Alkmaar-born merchant who was interested in African and Asian trade. His company traded with the East Indies prior to the formation of the VOC in 1602; he was important in the formation of the VOC; and thereafter served as a director of its Enkhuizen department (Van Brakel, *De Hollandsche Handelscompagnieën der Zeventiede Eeuw*, pp. 3, 103; Elias, *De Vroedschap van Amsterdam*, I, p. 125). Steenhuyssen was mentioned in Van Wassenaer (*Historisch verhael*, October 1624: f. 28r) as the patron of the Loango-based factor Joost Gerritsz Lijnbaen (see entry for 22 April 1612).

the 27th day. We passed the [equatorial] line, and we at midday measured the latitude of 40 minutes north. In the evening we came into the trade winds.

April [1609]

the 3rd day. We were at midday at the latitude of 4 degrees 25 minutes, and we got the north-east wind.

the 13th day. A flying fish came flying into the chest of our provost, and after we had looked around for the fish for a good while, it was discovered that it was hidden in his shirt.

May [1609]

the 10th day. We sounded a depth of seventy fathoms. We were at the latitude of 50 degrees 30 minutes.

the 13th day. We sighted Leser [= Lizard] and, from then on, the English coast.

the 14th day. Together we came to Plijmuyden [= Plymouth] and anchored at West Confar.[1]

the 22nd day. Went again to sea but because of the contrary wind we were forced to run to Doortmuyden [= Dartmouth], and ran in on the 24th. In the evening I met Abraham Vinck, a painter, in the Emden Inn, who had come with his wife from Rossel [= La Rochelle] to go live in Amsterdam.

the 26th day. Went again out of Doortmuyden [= Dartmouth] .

the 28th day. We anchored together in the Hoofden [= 'The Heads'[2]]. Gerrit Pieterssen set a new rode but, because it was not fixed to the bitt, it passed through the hawse-hole.

June [1609]

the 4th day. We arrived at Texssel [= Texel], thanks to God. I sailed immediately towards land and then went towards Amsterdam.

[1] An anchorage outside Plymouth Bay (Ratelband, *Reizen naar West-Afrika*, p. 38 n. 2).

[2] See p. 25 n. 1.

the 5th day. In the morning I entered Amsterdam and went to the house of my uncle, Hans van den Barghe, where I found my mother, Paulus's uncle, his wife, and Pieter van Ray,[1] my cousin, who had all just come visiting from Hamborch [= Hamburg]. Learned that my niece Grietken had married Dirck Bruggen.[2] Mayken, her sister, was married to Niellier. Jeronimus van den Barghe was married to the niece of Lenert Ray.[3] So, thanks to God, the numbers of our family were now much increased.

[1] Ray was a sugar-refiner (Ratelband, *Reizen naar West-Afrika*, p. 39 n. 3).

[2] Another sugar-refiner (Ibid., p. 39 n. 5)

[3] Lenert Ray was a Limburg-born merchant in spices, and a banker who did his business on the Barnsteeg in Amsterdam, and was commissioned by the Amsterdam department of the VOC (Ibid., p. 39 n. 6).

Journal in Brief of My Second Voyage from Amsterdam to Angola as Chief Factor with the ship *Nassou*, I mean *Mauritius*[1] with Master Pieter Cornelissen Mannis, fifty lasts in size, armed with eight *goetelingen,* six *steenstucken* and twenty-one sturdy men

September 1609

the 16th day. In the afternoon I left Amsterdam for Texssel [= Texel] in the company of four of our *bewindthebbers*[2] to sail with the first suitable wind that God should give.

the 17th day. In the afternoon we raised our anchor and sailed with a north-east wind out to sea. May Almighty God provide us with luck and a safe journey.

Left Texssel [=Texel] for Angola with the ship *Mauritius*

the 21st day. We anchored leeward of Duyns [= The Downs, near Dover] and next to four enormous royal ships, namely the admiral and vice-admiral of England who were bound for the Spanish coast.[3] We remained anchored between three castles or redoubts which sit on the beach.

the 22nd day. Went ashore with the master and the junior merchant,

[1] A different VOC-owned ship with the same name (honouring the Dutch *stadhouder*, Prince Maurits) sank off Cape Lopez in March 1609 on its return voyage from the East Indies. See the archaeological survey in L'Hour *et al.*, *Le Mauritius: la mémoire engloutie*.

[2] *Bewindhebbers* were company directors; see the Introduction.

[3] Ratelband identifies these English ships as the *Anne Royal*, *Nonsuch*, *Assurance*, and *Speedwell*, which were all under the command of Sir William Monson, admiral of the Narrow Seas (Ratelband, *Reizen naar West-Afrika*, p. 40 n. 1).

Was in the town Sandwiets [=Sandwich] in England

and went together on foot to Santwiets [= Sandwich], which lies a mile inland. Many Flemings live here and most of the baize trade takes place there. In the evening I returned to the coast on horseback.

the 24th day. We all went to Doeveren [= Dover], which was two long miles away. There is good trade in this town. Looked at the castle from the outside and rode back to the coast in the evening.

the 28th day. With a north-west wind, we raised anchor and sailed in God's name.

October [1609]

the 2nd day. We decided to run into Vaelmuyden [= Falmouth] because our ship was so leaky. I went immediately ashore and rode with the chief factor to a little village named Perijn [= Penryn], which lies around an English mile inland.

the 4th day. I was summoned to the castle by the governor who wished to see our ship's certificate of registry, but because we had left so suddenly, we had brought none. The governor ordered us to remain anchored so that our ship could be searched.

the 6th day. The commander of the castle came aboard with captain Moy Lambert[1] and searched the ship. Once they were satisfied, they returned ashore. We raised our anchor after midday and went to sea in God's name.

the last day. We arrived at Capo Verde. In the evening we anchored near the mainland, before Refusco [= Rufisque]. Found here two French [ships] which stayed here and traded. Anchored at five fathoms. Three canoes came immediately alongside us.

November [1609]

the first day. In the early morning I went ashore to fish with our

[1] Ratelband identified this captain's nickname, Moy Lambert ('pretty Lambert'), as an alias for Commander Lambrecht Hendrixsz, who patrolled the English Channel for pirates and privateers (ibid., p. 41 n. 3).

seine.[1] Before daybreak I was again back aboard. Raised our anchor and sailed to Portodaele [= Portudal] where we arrived in the evening in the roadstead, thanks to God. I went immediately ashore where I found our [man] Hans de Haesse.[2] Learned from this Portuguese that two days before our arrival, two galleys and a caravel from Portugal had come there, and were bound for Mijnne [= Elmina] castle.[3] Around thirty Portuguese and mestizos stay here.

Came to Portodaele [=Portudal] for the third time

the 5th day. A yacht arrived here with master Heyn Classen and merchant Jan Classen.

the 6th day. After we had taken in water and food, I also bought an ox for seven iron bars, and then we went under sail.

the 2nd of January 1610

the 2nd day. In the morning before daybreak we were near St Thome [= São Tomé]. The northern point lay east and south of us. We sailed above the cape [= Cape Lopez] with a nice breeze, but as we were coming close to the shore, it went dead calm and we were heaved towards land by the strong swells. Close to land we found no ground on which to anchor, so that if God Almighty had not provided us with a land wind, we surely would have lost the ship there. The natives were already piously waiting for us in order to congratulate us, because we were so close that we could call to them.

Saw Ste. Thome [São Tomé] and nearly lost the ship there

the 7th day. We arrived again at the Cabo de Loop Gonsalvis [= Cape

[1] Dutch ships carried various sorts of fishing tackle with which the crew could catch fresh food, scout out possible commercial possibilities and, in general, fight boredom while at sea. The sort of net Van den Broecke used here was an efficient tool to encircle and trap minnows in small streams. Elsewhere in the manuscript Van den Broecke alludes to the use of cast nets used in shallow, open waters (see entry for 29 March 1608), as well as hooks and lines, nets, and harpoons used to snare fish while at sea (see entries for 16 March 1609 and 1 December 1611).

[2] Van den Broecke met with Hans de Haese on his previous trip. See entry for 6 February 1608.

[3] This convoy of a supply ship and two galleys arrived at Elmina on 22 December 1609 to deliver news of the twelve-year Dutch-Iberian truce. The Governor of São Jorge da Mina, Duarte de Lima, disregarded the notice and sent the two galleys out to patrol the coast and prey on Dutch ships (Vogt, *Portuguese Rule on the Gold Coast*, p. 161).

Came to anchor at the Cabo de Lobo Gonsalvis [=Cape Lopez] for the third time

Lopez]. Found a sloop here from the coast of Guinea, with a certain Doede Floris as master.[1] Found also a small French ship in the bay which the French had purposely beached. Its principal left with Claes Jorissen from Rotterdam, and the other Frenchmen were still there, in idleness. We found two anchors there, which we took, and with a good length of rope as well. I burned this little ship for its old iron.

the 14th day. In the morning we raised our anchor and went to sea with a land wind.

the 17th day. We came to anchor a good distance away south of the cape because there was no wind. Anchored at eleven fathoms next to a cape that is very similar to the Cabo de Lop [= Cape Lopez]. The coast here runs south-east by east and south-south-east. This place was to my reckoning ten to twelve from the aforementioned Cabo Lop [= Cape Lopez]. Found that the current ran hard around the south.

the 23rd day. At noon we measured the latitude of 3 degrees 10 minutes. Inland it is very high.

the 24th day. In the morning [were] close to shore. At noon we were at the latitude of 3 degrees 16 minutes. Had here only a poor coast,[2] but high surrounding land with large, high hills. Anchored in the evening at thirteen fathoms, nearly a half mile from land. Found that little or no current comes from the north. The coast here runs mostly south-east and south-east by east.

Arrived at Majomba [=Mayoumba]

the 26th day. We arrived at Maiomba [= Mayoumba], which lies at

[1] On 17 May 1609 a convoy of three of Elias Trip's ships, the *Jagher*, the *Hasewindt* and the *Brack*, left for Mouri under the command of master Doede Florissen. In late September the convoy was on the Guinea coast when it was overwhelmed by soldiers from Elmina Castle attacking from African canoes (as Elmina had no ships of its own until the Portuguese galleys mentioned above arrived there months later). They seized both cargo and some prisoners, but obviously not Florissen himself (Klein, *De Trippen in de 17e Eeuw*, pp. 141–3; Vogt, *Portuguese Rule on the Gold Coast*, pp. 160–61).

[2] *Al slechten strandt.* The meaning of the sentence is that coastal areas were low, level, and unremarkable, but bordered by more distinctive elevations in the interior.

the latitude of 3 degrees 20 minutes. It curves inward there. There lie two visible shoals near shore. We anchored at seven fathoms on good, sandy ground. If you sit right in the roadstead, you want to keep the south corner south-south-west of you, and the north corner west by north. I immediately sailed with our boat towards land, well armed, and found here a mulatto named Lowies Mendis, who bought up all the redwood he could get for the *contractadoor*[1] of Loanda de Ste Pauwel [= Luanda]. This wood is known as *taccoela*[2] by the natives. Along the entire coast, they mostly use this for smearing on their bodies. There are elephant's tusks here as well, but not in such abundance as in Loango or other places around there.

the 27th day. I bought four elephant's tusks weighing 74 lb for four *covados*[3] of *palmillio*[4] from the natives. From the aforementioned mulatto I also bought 361 lb of tusks at 4,000 *réis* a *quintal*, and 200 pieces of *taccola* to take to Congo, where it is in great demand. Raised our anchor in the evening and sailed for Loango. The current was very strong out of the south, which was not in the least bit surprising.

the 30th day. In the morning we came to the roadstead of Loango, Arrived for

[1] In the Portuguese empire, *contratadores* paid bullion to the Crown for year-long monopoly concessions (*contrato*) to trade in slaves, ivory, the red dye-wood known as takula, salt, and tobacco. Lowies Mendis may have been a sub-contracting client, or *avençador*, who received working capital in the form of textiles, shells, salt, etc., from his *contratador* in Luanda and to whom he remitted supplies of redwood at rates that were usually below-market. Suppliers like Mendis seized the opportunity to work surreptitiously outside these contracts by doing a side-business in products for which they held no rights to trade and by selling goods to foreign merchants and interlopers who offered higher purchase prices rather than meet their obligations to the *contratadores*. In the early 17th century Dutch merchants like Van den Broecke (see his deal with Mendis below) made the most significant challenge to Portuguese monopoly contracts (Clark, 'Black Gold: The Portuguese Slave Trade from Angola').

[2] Takula (*Pterocarpus soyauxii*, and *P. tinctorius* Welw.) was principally produced in the area of Sette Cama and then bulked at Mayomba for shipment (Martin, *External Trade of the Loango Coast*, pp. 39–40; Jones, *German Sources*, p. 26 n. 28).

[3] The Portuguese *côvado* was a unit of length similar to other nations' 'ell'. See the appendix on 'Weights, Measures'.

[4] Blue cloth from Portugal.

the second time in Loango with the ship *Mauritius*

thanks to God. I went immediately ashore to speak with the king.[1] Once ashore, I went to the house of the factor Jaques van der Voorde, who had come here with a bark and was on the account of both of the companies. The aforementioned bark lay near the river Congo. I returned aboard in the evening with the factor Jaques van der Voorde without having spoken to the king. Learned that the same Van der Voorde had bought over 296 *quintals* of elephant's tusk at 3,500 *réis* a *quintal*. Also [heard] that blue duffels[2] were now most in demand.

the last day. I went ashore with a present for the king and his nobles, and only my audience with him at midday. I presented the king with a red and a black piece of *vierloodt*, and he gave me licence to trade here without restriction. He gave us lodging in the house of a great nobleman, named Mani Macase. I presented each of the four principal nobles, namely Manni Vasja, Manni Macase, Manni Queboute, and Mannij Quingie[3] with eight ells of *vierlooden*.

February [1610]

the 8th day. I went with a cargo of twenty pieces of cloth and other small *munidentien*[4] to the town Bansa de Loango [= Mbanza Loango], to the house of the king's mother. The boatswain who stayed with me was named Willem Barentssen.

the 14th day. After I had stowed aboard 785 lb of elephant's tusks, I sent the ship to the Congo river with the merchant Cornelis Arrentssen.

the 28th day. A Portuguese bark arrived here, coming from Loanda de Sant Pauwel [= Luanda], to load *labongos,* [with which] to pay the

[1] This 'king' was presumably the *mani* Loango. For the etymology of the *mani* title in Loango, see Martin, *External Trade of the Loango Coast*, p. 3, n. 3; also Samuel Brun's remarks about *mani* names (Jones, *German Sources*, p. 50).

[2] A blanket fabric with a nap on both sides, and made from low-grade woollen cloth. The name derives from Duffel, a town near Antwerp.

[3] These names do not correspond to the names of the four lordships of Loango given in Battel: Manicaye, Manibock, Manisalag, and Manicabango (in Ravenstein, *Strange Adventures*, pp. 49–50); nor to the four given later in Dapper (*Naukeurige Bescrhijvinghe*, pp. 145–6,159–60): Mani Bomma, Manimamba, Mani-Belor, and Maconda.

[4] Portuguese, 'provisions'.

soldiers who were stationed in the *conquista* of Massagan [= Massangano] on behalf of the king of Spain.[1]

the 29th day. I saw a seal[2] similar in appearance to a seal in Holland, except that its legs were a little shorter and only a *span*[3] long. Otherwise it is almost identical in its head, nose, ears, body and tail. This aforementioned seal had lain on the beach in the sun stinking for at least four days, so that the worms were coming out of it in great numbers. It was brought as a great present to the king, who sent me a quarter of it, and which cost me more than one quarter ell of cloth to have quietly carried off, because it reeked so terribly. With the rest of this tasty seal the king made other good friends.[4]

Illustration of a seal in Loango.

[blank space in the manuscript]

March [1610]

the 16th day. The ship the *Merman* from Amsterdam arrived here this morning. The master was Jan Pieterssen from Hooren [= Hoorn][5] and the factor was Fredrick Janssen from Edam, and they were from

[1] The Portuguese fort Massangano, located near the confluence of the Kwanza and Lukala rivers, was the focal point of the colonial government's assault on the Mbundu kingdom of Ndongo (Birmingham, *Trade and Conflict in Angola*, pp. 54–5, 60; Miller, *Kings and Kinsmen: Early Mbundu States in Angola*, p. 179). The Iberian term *conquista* ('conquest') refers not only to military assault, but more generally to the process of formal expansion of economic, political, and moral influence over non-Christian communities; on the idea of the *conquista*, see Gibson, 'Conquest and So-Called Conquest in Spain and Spanish America'.

[2] Van den Broecke wrote that he saw a *zeehondt* (lit. 'sea dog'), which means a seal in modern Dutch. It is possible that he meant to write *waterhondt* (lit. 'water dog'), an old word for shark as well as an old description for canine retrievers. For De Marees's description of a canine *waterhondt*, see Van Dantzig and Jones, *Pieter de Marees*, p.143.

[3] The Dutch *span* was about 20 centimetres

[4] If this *zeehondt* was indeed a canine animal, Van den Broecke's revulsion was not unique: the consumption of dogs and rotting flesh shocked many European observers, including De Marees (Van Dantzig and Jones, *Pieter de Marees*, pp. 41, 128–9), Brun (Jones, *German Sources*, p. 87), and Müller (ibid., pp. 209–10).

[5] Jan Pieterssen was the 'patron' (meaning owner?) of the ship that Samuel Brun took to Loango in 1611 (Naber, *Samuel Brun's Schiffarten*, p. 1)

the company of Lucas van der Venne[1] and Sijmon Willemssen Noms.[2]

the 19th day. I and the chief factor on the bark, named Jaques van der Voorde, went aboard the ship the *Merman,* to see if we could make a contract with the other, because the blacks had already begun to make trouble. The same evening I purchased also from the inhabitants fifteen *quintals* of elephant's tusk at 4,000 *réis* per *quintal.*

May [1610]

the 2nd day. This morning the bark the *Marcurius,* with merchant Jaques van der Voordt and master Jan Gerritsen Tuynpadt, sailed for the Fatherland, loaded with 63,000 lb of elephant's tusks. May God Almighty safely guide her.

the 17th day. A ship named *Samson* arrived here from Amsterdam. The master was Gerret Pieterssen from Hooren. It came here to trade as well. Brought me news that our ship *Mauritius* lay at Cacongo [= Kakongo], [and was] very desolate, with many sick people, and that the master Pieter Cornelissen had gone upriver to go to trade with a Portuguese renegade named Manuel da Costa.

the 27th day. Our ship came to the roadstead here. I immediately had stowed all the elephant's tusks that I had traded.

June [1610]

the 2nd day. I fell very ill.

July [1610]

the last day. When I had recovered a bit, thank God, I again took on board a nice batch of tusks and then sent the ship again to the Cacongo River to fetch our master Pieter Cornelissen.

[1] Lucas van der Venne was an Amsterdam merchant and sugar-refiner (Ratelband, *Reizen naar West-Afrika*, p. 46 n. 3). He was also mentioned in Van Wassenaer (*Historisch verhael*, October1624: f. 28r) as an investor in African trade; see entry for 22 April1612, and the Introduction, p. 8 n. 2.

[2] Simon Willemssen Nooms was also an Amsterdam merchant, interested primarily in the Guinea trade (Elias, *De Vroedschap van Amsterdam*, I, p. 431).

October [1610]

the 24th day. In the morning the aforementioned ship the *Samson* departed with Jan Louwerssen as factor and master, replacing the deceased master Gerret Pieterssen. It carried around 220 *quintals* of elephant's tusks from the coast, of which twenty-eight *quintals* were from the river of Seti,[1] which lies at the latitude of 2 degrees 28 minutes, between Mayomba [= Mayoumba] and Cabo de Lopo Gonsalvis [= Cape Lopez]. At this time of year it is very difficult to enter the river, because in the dry season it gets silted up by the sea. The blacks there desire most of all *lijwaet massa ma[?-]omba* or large *rosados.*[2] While stowing the tusks here in Loango, the natives had stolen more

[1] This probably refers to the river that flows into Lagune Ndogo. Sette-Cama is the name of a town on the south side of the peninsula that separates the lagoon from the ocean.

[2] *De swarten begerren aldaer al mest lijwaet massa ma[?-]omba ofte groote rosados.* This passage is difficult to interpret. The middle part of the word *ma[?-]omba* is smudged in the manuscript. Also, the sentence's construction and punctuation leave it ambiguous how many different trade items are listed here – three items or two, and perhaps an appositive phrase giving two names for the same item. Some aspects are identifiable: *lijwaet* is certainly linen, and *groote rosados* are large, round beads, like those of the rosary (see Jones, *Brandenburg Sources*, p. 318). I suspect that *massa ma[?-]omba* and *groote rosados* are two names for the same trade beads, with the first being the local name and the latter being Dutch. If so, the local name was perhaps constructed from the Mayombe words for beads (*misaa*) and prayer (*masamba*, in Bittremieux, *Mayombisch Idioticon*). See also the Kikongo *masàmbúlu*, 'holy, sacramental objects' (in Swartenbroeckx, *Dictionnaire Kikongo et Kituba-Français*, p. 304). So understood, the sentence would thus read, 'The blacks there desire most of all linen [and] *massa ma[?-]omba*, also known as large *rosados*.' Alternatively, but I think less likely, *massa ma[?-]omba* may have been describing the preceding *lijwaet*. One of Van den Broecke's contemporaries, Samuel Brun, described *masa* as the local word for palm oil (Jones, *German Sources*, p. 52, with n. 40). Might *lijwaet massa ma[?-]omba* have been a high-quality cloth, likened to linen (*lijwaet*), made in Loango from the fibres (*misâsa*, in Swartenbroeckx, *Dictionnaire Kikongo*) of the oil palm *(masamba,* in Pechuel-Loesche, *Die Loango-Expedition ausgesant von der Deutschen*)? For such cloth, see Brun (Jones, *German Sources*, p. 50). On a previous trip to Loango, the *mani* Loango gave Van den Broecke 'palm cloths' to take and trade on his behalf up north; see entry for 1 May 1608. It would be very unusual to make cloth from fibre from the oil (as opposed to the raffia) palm, however. Finally, Van den Broecke may have been somewhat unclear himself about the items, as the entire passage about trade at 'Seti' seems secondhand, probably reported to him by the *Samson*'s Jan Louwerssen.

than eleven *quintals* of the best and biggest tusks, which was a great loss for its owners.

November [1610]

the 9th day. Our Willem Barrentssen died, who had accompanied me ashore.[1] I had him taken out to sea, because the blacks would not allow him to be buried on land in any way. They said that because of this [=otherwise], no more rain would fall.[2]

the 20th day. The rainy season began in Loango and on the entire coast. Sometimes it rained continuously for three days at a time.[3] The same day I caught a chameleon, as big as a lizard and a foot long. These animals live solely off of the wind[4] and their bodies will assume and change into whatever colour you place them on.

A chameleon in Loango.

[blank space in the manuscript]

the last day. The king's sister, named Manni Lombo,[5] invited me to sleep with her.[6] She gave me an elephant's tusk of 90 lb with vegetables like *bannanus* [= plantains], limes, pineapples, beans, and other such fruits. Sent me around eighteen men with a Portuguese hammock to carry me and accompany me to her town that lies about a half day's travel inland.

[1] This ship's mate had been to Mbanza Loango with Van den Broecke; see entry for 8 February 1610.

[2] Battel related that after the death of a Portuguese trader and his burial on land, there had been a delay in the onset of the rainy season; only with the trader's disinterment and burial at sea, did the rains finally come (Ravenstein, *Strange Adventures*, p. 51).

[3] *Over een boech* is a 17th-century colloquialism meaning 'in succession' or 'consecutively'. I have inserted a similar expression in modern English.

[4] That is, chameleons are rarely seen eating. That they lived solely on air was an oft-repeated European story.

[5] See also Battel (Ravenstein, *Strange Adventures*, p. 50).

[6] Battel wrote that the *mani* Lombo 'is the highest and chief woman in all the land. She maketh choice of her husband, and when she is weary of him she putteth him away, and taketh another' (Ibid., p. 50).

January 1611 in Loango

the 18th day. In the morning the bark the *Mercurius* arrived here in the roadstead, coming out of Holland from Amsterdam, and was on the account of our *mesters*. The master was named Gerret Dirckxssen Os and the senior factors were Jaques van der Voorde and Jacop Seggerssen. The junior factor was Adam Vermeullen and the mate was Arris Janssen from Wormer.[1] This master had previously been the master of the ship the *Neptunis*. They had been under way for just three months and three days.[2]

April [1611]

the 9th day. I took my leave of the king of Loango, now that I had lain still here for fifteen months. He presented me with sixteen beautiful elephant's tusks which weighed well over 1,000 lb, and also one leopard's skin,[3] twelve pieces of *bondo*,[4] which are held in great esteem here, at which many natives were amazed, as he had never presented so many of these to anyone before.

Left Loango for the second time and sailed again for the Fatherland with the ship *Mauritius*

the 13th day. I left land and went aboard with my baggage. I had been gone for less than half an hour when the king himself came in person with his entire following to the place where I had stayed, [and] where he hoped to still find me. He sent aboard two more tusks for me which together weighed more than 180 lb. For as long as I had been here in Loango, the king had never been more than a musket-shot away from his court. I had to promise the nobleman who brought me the tusks, that I would return. In the evening we raised our anchor and sailed in God's name.

the 16th day. We arrived in Majomba [= Mayoumba] to get a batch of redwood there, known as *taccola*.

[1] Van den Broecke made his first tip to 'Angola' aboard the *Neptunnis*, with Aris Janssen as the master; see title heading for 14 November 1607.

[2] Van den Broecke had noted the departure of this bark, the *Mercurius*, in the entry for 2 May 1610.

[3] In Loango, leopards were symbols of royalty and their skins were worn only by kings and nobility (Martin, *External Trade of the Loango Coast*, p. 21 n. 3).

[4] Bondo was the finest cloth made by raffia weavers exclusively for the king (Jones, *German Sources*, p. 52; Martin, *External Trade of the Loango Coast*, p. 37).

the 19th day. At midday we got a hard breeze south-west by west with such hard gusts that our rope broke into pieces, and we only just got another one into place, or else we would have been in the breakers.

Left Majombe [=Mayoumba] for the Fatherland

the 26th day. Near midday we raised our anchor and set our course out to sea, for home. May God Almighty bless us with a safe trip.

May [1611]

the 15th day. We passed the equator.

the 21st day. At the latitude of 5 degrees 3 minutes we got the north-east wind and set a north-west by south[1] course.

July [1611]

Had ground and saw land which we presumed was Leser [=Lizard]

the 16th day. At the latitude of 49 degrees 35 minutes we sounded a depth of sixty fathoms, with gritty sand and *sorlis*[2] ground. At night we sounded again and found only fifty-five fathoms. At sunset we saw land lying across from us, which we presumed to be Lesert [= Lizard]. I ordered that we would sail right into the Channel.

the 24th day. In the morning we came before Schevelinghen [= Scheveningen] and were at around eight o'clock before Sandtwoordt [= Zandvoort]. I ordered a shot to be fired. A pilot came immediately aboard, who took me ashore for eight guilders, so that I arrived thanks to God in the evening outside of Amsterdam, by way of Haerlem [= Haarlem], where I had all the luck of finding my uncle Jasper van Ray.

the 25th day. Thanks to God our master also ran in safely at Texel.

the 27th day. Our master arrived at Amsterdam loaded with 1,800 pieces of red wood, called *tacola*, which we had brought to do a test to see if it could be used by the dyers. Furthermore there was in the same ship at least 65,000 lb of elephant's tusks which I had traded in

[1] Must be an error for 'north-west by north'.

[2] It is not clear what this means. They may have found bottom soil which was like the soil of the Scilly Isles, the Dutch 'Sorles Eilanden' (Ratelband, *Reizen naar West-Afrika*, p. 57 n. 5).

Loango, Cacongo [= Kakongo], Schonnio [= Sonyo], Maiomba [= Mayoumba] and Cascais.

August [1611]

the last day. I travelled from Amsterdam to Hamborch [= Hamburg] to go to visit my parents, where I arrived, thanks to God, on September 7th.

the 20th day.[1] Travelled again from Hamborch [= Hamburg] to Amsterdam, to sail again to Angola as chief factor.

[1] Since the preceding entry is for the last day of the month, this must be a mistake for the 20th of the next month, September.

Journal of My Third Voyage to Angola as Chief Factor with the ship that I was with in Loango the first time, but now renamed the *Son*[1] (with Master Jan Janssen Backer from Amsterdam), ninety lasts in size and armed with ten *gootelinghen*, six *steenstucken*, and thirty sturdy men

the 7th of November [= October[2]] 1611

the same day. I travelled in the company of the *bewindthebbers* from Amsterdam to Texsel [= Texel] to sail to Angola from there with the first good wind that God Almighty should give.

[blank space in the manuscript]

the 25th day. We formed a convoy with a Guinea-bound ship and three others which were bound for the Canaries. We were vice-admiral, a ship from Enckhuyssen [= Enkhuizen] was admiral, and Sent Sendtssen from Amsterdam was third-in-command.

the 30th day. We went to sea from Texsel [= Texel] with a north-east wind and in the company of more than eighty ships.[3] Our master was named Jan Janssen Backer from Amsterdam. The junior factors were Anthonij Beucelaer, Heyn Classen, and Marten van Colck from Deventer.

Sailed in the Name of God with the ship the *Son* to Angolla

[1] The ship was originally named the *Neptunis*.

[2] Van den Broecke made a mistake here, placing November before October (see below). The names of the two months should obviously be reversed.

[3] Most of these ships were probably headed somewhere else than Angola (to Brazil, to South American salt pans, to the East Indies), but they left as a large convoy to guard against privateers on their common route through the English Channel and along the Spanish coast.

October [=November 1611]

the 12th day. We spotted Portosant [= Porto Santo] and the island of Maderien [= Madeira]. We parted company after we had visited our admiral, which was from Enckhuyssen [= Enkhuizen]. On the same day, in the morning, a boatswain on the admiral-ship fell from the flagpole over a railing, and from there he hit the corner of the mainsail, and he wasn't hurt at all.

A man fell from the flagpole without injury

the 22nd day. In the morning at sunrise we found ourselves to the west, right beside Sante Croes [= Santa Cruz] on the ....[1] side of the island Teneriffa [= Tenerife] and, as we could see in from the open sea, there were five ships which were doing their best to get close to us. We presumed that they didn't have good intentions, so therefore we decided to run below the castle. Before we came below the castle, the vice-admiral [of the threatening ships] was so close to us that we could easily shoot at it. I had one shot fired at it, and just as the shot was fired, the castle too let off a shot at it, upon which they immediately went out to sea. We dropped anchor and immediately the *augissel*[2] from land came on board to search the ship and to ask what our cargo was, from whence we came, and where we wanted to go. Answered him that we came under the orders of the merchant Gerret Veen and that we were loaded with beams and planks. He wanted the master to come immediately ashore because he thought we were freebooters.[3] This *augusiel* told us that these aforementioned ships had cruised there for more than three weeks, off and on; also that the previous day they had taken a Portuguese caravel coming from Lisbonna [= Lisbon], and its crew set ashore at De Orratava [= La Oratava].[4] The admiral was a English ship armed with thirty cannon and 150 men. The remaining ships were likewise

[1] The ellipse occurs in the original. Perhaps Van den Broecke intended to look to other sources, personal and published, to fill in the directional details he forgot here.

[2] Portuguese *auguazil* (alternatively, *alguazil*), a generic term for a minor official, particularly in the judicial services.

[3] The *auguazil*'s accusation was probably as disingenuous as the ship's reported cargo and destination. He was soliciting a bribe from the ship, to let it leave unharmed.

[4] La Oratava, a town on the west coast of the island.

fitted, so it was indeed a miracle that we had escaped from their clutches. Our master stayed ashore for the night to deliver the letters to the merchant Gerret Veen. Lay anchored at eighteen fathoms and the ship at twenty-two, that is how steep it is here.

the 23rd day. Our master returned aboard with a servant of Gerret Veen, named Pieter Hendrickxssen Verwind, and the *augusiel* to search the ship on behalf of the Inquisition. Gave him four hams and four cheeses for the governor of the castle. I went ashore in the evening and rode on horseback (with a *Duytsse*[1] merchant friend of Gerret Veen named Pieter Galliet) to the town named Allagonne [= La Laguna], which lies more than a mile inland, and went to the house of Gerret Veen, who wasn't there because he had already ridden to De Orrata [= La Oratava] because of his other ships, which had accompanied us here. In the evening I went to visit Pieter Galliet, who had married an exceptionally beautiful Portuguese woman.

Was in the town of Allagone [=La Laguna] on the island Tersera [=Terceira], I mean, Teneriff [=Tenerife]

the 27th day. After we had bought victuals, including lemons, grapes, onions, one *pijp*[2] of wine and other similar things, and the ships were out of sight, and we heard continuous shooting near De Orratave [= La Oratava], we finally sailed in the Name of God, shortly before evening.

November [1611]

the 22nd day. We floated quietly at the latitude of 7 degrees 16 minutes north of the equator and by reckoning about sixty miles from shore. In the evening we caught a quail.

December [1611]

the first day. It was still dead calm. Caught great numbers of fish, such as albacore, snook, dorado, and baskets of small fry which we made into good anchovies. [I] caught an albacore six and a half feet

[1] On the meaning of *Duytsse*, see pp. 36 n. 1, 45 n. 2, above.

[2] A *pijp* measured liquid volume and was equal to two hogsheads (*oxhoofden*). One *pijp* was divided into 3 *aamen*, each of which was divided into 64 *stoopen*. Converted to modern, metric units, a *pijp* is equivalent to about 460 litres (Posthumus, *Inquiry into the History of Prices*, pp. lii–liii; Jones, *Brandenburg Sources*, p. 318).

long and four and three quarters feet thick. I shot a snook seven and a half feet long with the *ellagaer*.[1] These snook are thought to be the most delicious fish that you can catch in the sea. At midday measured a latitude of 5 degrees 20 minutes.

An albacore six and quarter feet long and four and three quarters [feet] thick.

[blank space in the manuscript]

Stopped and released a Portuguese bark below the equator

the 16th day. It was still dead calm, with much rain. Before midday, saw a sail behind us [and] sailed towards it. On coming close we had him strike his sails, and had the master from it come aboard, who was a Portuguese, and who had sailed with this bark from Lisbonna [= Lisbon] and wanted to go to Ste Thome [= São Tomé]. The aforementioned master was named Philipe Loppes Moreno. I invited him to be our guest in the evening, presented him with a cheese, and let him return unharmed back aboard. His cargo was wine, pans,[2] and hides, as well as other trade-goods of little importance.[3] He presented me with a batch of fruit preserves. At noon, we measured a latitude of 4 degrees 50 minutes.

A flying-fish flew into the hawse-hole

the 29th day. After we had lain becalmed, for the most part, since the11th of November, and had advanced what proved to be only 5 degrees, we got a fairly good breeze. At midday we measured a latitude of 1 degree 55minutes. In the evening a flying fish, a span long, flew into the hawse-hole.

January 1612 at sea

the 2nd day. In morning, at dawn, we saw the island of St. Thome [= São Tomé] around five miles north-east from us.

[1] A small, forked harpoon.

[2] Portuguese traders sold mostly brasswares (basins, pots, manillas), at least some of which were melted down and reworked locally by African craftsmen (Elbl, 'Portuguese Trade with West Africa', pp. 367–8, 396–405). Dutch traders entered the Guinea trade in pans by offering the same range of various vessel shapes, but they were relatively high-quality German copperwares (Ratelband, *Vijf Dagregisters van het Kasteel São Jorge da Mina*, pp. xcviii–cviii).

[3] This description of Mereno's cargo suggests that he was only a petty merchant who had not yet procured a full cargo to take back to Lisbon.

the 5th day. In the evening we came below the Cabo de Loep [= Cape Lopez], in the roadstead. Found here a Guinea-faring ship named the *Ouden Man,* with master Ewoudt Hendrickxssen.[1] They were preparing to leave for the Fatherland in company of three other ships which were yet to arrive from the coast.

Came to anchor at the Cabo de Loop [=Cape Lopez]

the 17th day. After we had put together our *speeljacht*[2] and had amply supplied ourselves here with fresh water, firewood,and other things, we sailed in the evening to Loango and Congo, in God's name. Left four ships lying here in the roadstead which were to return home in a convoy. [They were] namely the *Swarten Leuw,* with chief factor Rombout Pijls; the aforementioned ship the *Ouden Man*; with also a bark from Rotterdam; and the *Mermin.* These aforementioned ships altogether had no more than 520 lb of gold from the coast. As soon as we had rounded the cape, I sent our yacht to Loango with the junior factor Heyn Classen and five persons and provisioned for six weeks.

February [1612]

the 16th day. We arrived in the morning in the bay of Majomba [= Mayoumba]. I immediately sailed with a well-outfitted boat towards shore to determine what was going on here. On coming ashore I found a Portuguese here, my great friend Francisco Delmede Navero.

the 18th day. I ordered the junior factor Marten van Colck to go ashore with a cargo of about 400 guilders, and to accompany him was the sail-maker named Jacob Janssen Hartman. Raised our anchor in the evening and went to Loango.

Mayomba [= Mayoumba] lies at the latitude of 3 degrees 20 minutes. It is a beautiful bay which lies next to the land of the king of Loango. There are few elephant's tusks available but much red

[1] On Van den Broecke's first trip to Cape Verde, he worked as a junior factor under chief factor Ewoudt Hendricksz; see entry and annotation for 23 November 1605.

[2] *Speeljachten* were smaller and faster than yachts. A *speeljacht* was about 12 meters long with a single mast, although some had two, and had a glass cabin above deck. In the early 17th-century Netherlands, races were held for this type of pleasure craft. *Speeljachten* were also used for business travel on the inland waterways of the Netherlands (Unger, *Dutch Shipbuilding before 1800*, pp. 50–51).

wood, called *tacolla*, which is much in demand because the nobles rub it on themselves after it has been ground between two stones.

Arrived in Loango with the ship the *Son*

the 23rd day. In the evening we arrived, thanks to God, at Loango. Here we found our yacht, which had gotten here eleven days before our arrival. The junior factor, Adam Vermeulen,[1] and the senior factor of Pieter Brandt, named Albrech Damborch, came aboard. Altogether the bark had traded over 62,000 lb of elephant's tusks. Many of our crew were sick and suffering from scurvy.

Gave a present to the king of Loango

the 25th day. I brought a valuable present to the king of Loango, who was very pleased about my visit.[2]

the 26th day. I sent our yacht to Congo to inform the bark the *Marcurius* of our arrival. I brought a similar batch of merchandise ashore to trade.

March [1612]

The king himself came to our house

the 22nd day. The king of Loango himself came in person in my house with all of his nobles, which he never before had done for any other foreign nation, [and] at which all the natives were very amazed.

the 23rd day. I dispatched the bark the *Marcurius* to the bight of Benijn [=Benin] and the rivers of Gabon [= Gabon estuary] and Angre [= Corisco Bay], to trade there according to the instructions of our *heeren majoris*.[3]

the 29th day. I sent our ship the *Son* with the factor Jacob Segerssen to the Congo river to trade there.

April [1612]

the 22nd day. The yacht the *Maen* arrived here from Holland [and

[1] Junior factor Adam Vermeulen had been trading near Loango for thirteen months; for his arrival see entry for 18 January 1611.

[2] Van den Broecke's published books of 1634 elaborated on his arrival before the *mani* Loango; see the Introduction, pp. 15–16.

[3] *Heeren majoris* is a title describing the company directors. Typically it is used only to describe the directors of the West India Company (*Heeren XIX*) or East India Company (*Heeren XVII*), but see the Introduction, pp. 3–5.

came] under my command; our *majoris*[1] sent it to me to be used along the coast. This aforementioned yacht measured eighteen lasts. The factor, named Joost Gerretssen Lijnbaen,[2] had been on the Grain Coast in passing and there, with luck, filled the yacht with malaguetta, also known as grain, and 300 lb of elephant's tusks.

the 26th day. Pieter Brandt left the coast for home with around 50,000 lb of elephant's tusks which he had traded here and in Congo.

the 29th day. I went with the yacht the *Maen* from here to the Congo river to order everyone to get everything in order before I left for the Fatherland.

May [1612]

the 6th day. When we sailed around the hook of Cabinde [= Cabinda], the current was so strong that we were driven back. Anchored before Cabinde. I went ashore with a well-armed boat in order to find out if there was any way to pass overland through the kingdom of Mani Goi [= Ngoyo][3]. On coming ashore, was very well received by the natives, which gave me good hope.[4]

the 9th day. After I had got permission to go overland to the river, I travelled only with two blacks who carried me in a hammock and with two nobles for company and protection. Late that night I arrived in the town Bansa de Goi [= Mbanza Ngoyo], which I reckoned to lie five Dutch miles from the coast. In this place the king keeps his court, who immediately summoned me before him. Gave

Was before the King of Goi in his city and travelled through his land to Congo

[1] See p. 88 n. 3.

[2] Van Wassenaer recorded that Lijnbaen had maintained a presence in western Central Africa for 13 years as an agent for Hinlopen, Blommert, Steenhuysen, and Lucas van der Venne (Van Wassenaer, *Historisch verhael*, October 1624: f. 28r). Lijnbaen may have been one of Olfert Dapper's informants (see Jones, 'Decompiling Dapper', pp. 181–2).

[3] This route, overland and across the Congo River, would be the logical path to Sonyo if Portuguese ships were at Mpinda or in the mouth of the river, thereby preventing Dutch ships from trading there. For Luso-Dutch fighting on the Congo, see entry for 22 April 1608.

[4] Van den Broecke's fearful precautions were probably based on Ngoyo's hostile relationship with Loango, with whom the Dutch companies were increasingly close; see immediately following entry for 9 May 1612.

him the sum of eight ells of *vierlooden,* which pleased him very much. He at once let me stay in the house of one of his nobles, where I was well cared for with things that, according to custom, were all brought in from the royal court. This king is a very old and cruel man. He fights violently against the Insicussen[1] and is a great enemy of the king of Loango. This is a very fertile land with all sorts of *mantimentos* namely *mile masse* or Turkish wheat,[2] beans, *bannannus* [= plantains], apples [= oranges], and abundances of limes. Furthermore there are all sorts of animals such as sheep, goats, hart, buffalo, elephants, tigers, leopards, and other wild animals too. Chickens are also not lacking here. Bought twenty [chickens] for the price of a half of a *reael van achten* [= piece of eight].

the 10th day. In the morning the king sent me with a nobleman and six slaves to carry me in a hammock to the Congo river. In the evening I came into a town about four miles from Goi [= Mbanza Ngoyo], and had to stay in the house of the captain [=headman], because of the wild animals.

the 11th day. The king's slaves carried me to the Congo river, which was over two long miles away. On arriving there, I could see from atop a hill our ship lying at the hook of the Padron.[3] I hired a *prauw* for two ells of blue cloth[4] to bring me across this river.

Arrived in the city Schonho [=Mbanza Sonyo]

the 12th day. In the morning at daybreak I came aboard our ship, which sat at anchor inside the hook of the Padron. In the afternoon I arrived in the city of Schonho [= Mbanza Sonyo] where the junior factor Anthoni Classen Beukelaer and Jan Janssen van der Gaff lay [with their ship] and traded on behalf of our company.[5]

[1] The *Anziko*, the title of the ruler of the Tio kingdom, located north of the Malebo Pool.

[2] Two synonyms for maize. For the history of Dutch names for maize in the 17th and 18th centuries, see Wigboldus, 'De oudste Indonesische maïscultuur'.

[3] At this cape, the Portuguese had erected a pillar (*padrão*) to claim the area for God and country. It also served as a navigational aid for ships riding the Benguela current north.

[4] A popular colour (see entry for 30 January 1610).

[5] Thus indicating that Van den Broecke's company had negotiated with the *mani* Sonyo (perhaps on Van den Broecke's visit there, beginning 1 August 1608) to post factors there temporarily.

the 17th day. Now that I had put everything into order, I went aboard, ordered our anchor to be raised, and we sailed out of the Congo river in the name of God. Sailed to Cabinde [= Cabinda], where I had left the yacht the *Maen*.

June [1612]

the 5th day. Both of us[1] arrived in Loango.

the 18th day. I took my leave from the king Mani Loango, who gave me thirty-five elephant's tusks which weighed 1,905 lb, I had to promise him that I would return in person. I left the junior factor Heijn Classen here in my place.

the 21st day. Raised our anchor to sail in the Name of God to the Fatherland, but we first put in to Majomba [= Mayoumba]. Sailed out of the bay of Loango

the 22st day. We arrived at Majomba [= Mayoumba], thanks to God.

the 29th day. We sailed again, after I had taken aboard the elephant's tusks and redwood that the junior factor Marten van Colck had traded, and I had provided him with more goods to trade for an estimated period of three months.

July [1612]

the 14th day. In the evening master Jan Janssen Backer died. I made our first mate, Jan Reinssen, master in his place again. At midday we measured a latitude of 2 degrees 50 minutes south of the equator.

the 28th day. At the latitude of 11 degrees 30 minutes north of the equator, we got a north-east wind.

September [1612]

the 6th day. At the latitude of 49 degrees 28 minutes, we sounded for ground at a depth of sixty-five fathoms, which was white sand mixed with some black grains and small shells. Made our course east by north. Sounded for ground on the bank around 40 miles from Engelandtsende [=Land's End]

[1] That is, the *Son* and its yacht, the *Maen*.

the 7th day. In the morning we sailed north-east to sight land and see roughly where we were. When we had not seen any land by evening, we sailed due south and sounded for ground at a depth of forty-eight fathoms which was coarse sand mixed with little round pebbles and pieces of shells. From the depth and the sort of ground we had enough to conclude with some certainty that we were behind England in the channel of Bruston [= Bristol]. In the evening we sounded a depth of forty-five fathoms, which was white, fine sand mixed with some red. Took in our top-sails, and sounded the same depth in the middle of the night, which was soft, muddy ground. Took another tack, sailing south.

the 8th day. In the morning held our course to the south. At midday sighted the Sorlies [= Scilly Isles] roughly south-east by east from us while the wind was west and the weather was good. Went between the Sorlis [= Scilly Isles] and Engelandtsende [= Land's End]. Left the Seven Steen [= Seven Stones][1] lying on the lee side of us and The Wolf[2] on the weather side.

This error of falling into the channel of Bruston [= Bristol] is made because of a bank which lies directly before the mouth of the channel. Some say that it is at least 30 miles long and it is around sixty to sixty-five fathoms deep, with white fine sand mixed with some black. It lies around forty-five miles west and west by south of the Sorlies [= Scilly Islands]. Between this aforementioned bank and England you have again more than 100 fathoms depth and this depth is not very wide, which causes many to err.

With some small shells

the 16th day. We got a pilot on board,[3] and arrived safely at Texssel [= Texel] around noontime, thanks to God. I immediately went ashore [by boat].

the 17 day. In the early morning I arrived in Amsterdam.

the 18th day. The ship arrived before Amsterdam, loaded with

[1] A visible rock outcropping roughly 26 km due west of Land's End.

[2] Roughly 15 km south-south-west of Land's End.

[3] The pilot, or *loodtsman,* manoeuvred ships through the shallows between Noord-Holland and Texel, and through in the shallow waters of the Zuiderzee to reach Amsterdam.

96,000 lb of elephant's tusks and 800 pieces of red wood from Majomba [= Mayoumba], called *taccola* and also with eight lasts of malaguetta, at which the *Heeren Meesters* took great satisfaction and were very pleased.

Came home from Angola with the ship the *Son*

October [1612]

the 29th day. I left Amsterdam for Hamborch [= Hamburg], where I arrived on the 6th of November, thanks to God, and found my family doing well.

Description of the kingdom of Loango

The kingdom of Loango lies at the latitude of four and a half degrees from the equator on the coast of Africa. It is a very good bay for ships. But at the entrance to the aforementioned bay, on the south side, a bank of about a half mile runs parallel to the shore and it is about two and a half fathoms deep and is not wide. When you have passed it you have again five fathoms until you are around a *goeteling*-shot from land. And there you have red clay ground at three fathoms until you are around a musket-shot from land. But there is no need to sail so close to land. We never sat more than a *goeteling*-shot from land.

Loango is very easy to recognize by the red hills which lie before it, because on this entire coast, from de Cabo de Lobo Gonsalvis [= Cape Lopez] to the river of Congo, there are no hills like them. The coast runs from the aforementioned cape to Loango mostly south-east by south and south-south-east. Most of the year strong currents come here northwards, so that it is hardly possible to come up from below.[1] That is due to the prevailing south-east wind, which continually blows parallel to the coast. But in spite of that, there is always a west land-wind in the morning and in the afternoon the breeze off the sea, but this is very weak, so, again, if you want to come up from

[1] That is, to sail 'up' the coast, from north to south.

below, you must wait until the months of January, February, March and April, which is the *travoado*-season there. Only after this (although it is unnatural[1]) will you have strong northward currents. Some will say that this is not true, because during this season all of the rivers run very full and strong because of the continuous hard rains, but it seems that the wind arriving with the hard *travoados* usually has the upper hand.

In the year 1608, in the month of April, I sailed with the ship the *Neptunus* from the Cabo de Loop [= Cape Lopez] to Loango within in the timespan of fifteen days, which everyone thought to be a miracle because we were the first to have done this, although many foreign nations have tried to do the same.

In the year 1610 in January I did it again in sixteen days with the yacht *Mauritius* and in the year 1612 with the ship the *Sonne* in just fifteen days. So, since this time, no ships from the Fatherland have taken any other route. Before this they always crossed over to the coast of Bresiel [= Brazil] and usually sailed until they were at the latitude of 34 degrees.

The king keeps his residence less than a mile inland[2] in a town named Bansa de Loango [= Mbanza Loango], which lies on a very high hill and is an extremely pleasant location. The king's court covers almost half of the city and is surrounded by palm-wine trees. Inside the *pagger*[3] stand three or four large houses and another 250 small ones, in which live the king's wives, who are said to total more than 1,500 in number.[4] These aforementioned wives are distinguished by their ivory arm-rings, which they wear on their arms

[1] Meaning unclear: the pronoun 'it' probably refers to the *trovoado*-season, thus making a comparison between the maritime season in the north Atlantic, with which Van den Broecke was familiar, and that of the southern Atlantic. He encountered storms in the months of the northern summer, which he may have regarded as 'unnatural' because he associated those months with calm weather.

[2] Van Wassenaer (*Historisch verhael*, October 1624: f. 26v) put the distance at a half mile inland.

[3] *Pagger*, as written in the manuscript, is a Malay word for a 'fence' or 'barrier'.

[4] Battel counted more than 150 wives (Ravenstein, *Strange Adventures*, p. 45); Brun numbered them at 360 (Jones, *German Sources*, p. 51); and Van Wassenaer at 300 or 400 (*Historisch verhael*, October 1624: f. 27r).

along with much red paint. They are very closely guarded, and if any of them are found to be committing adultery, they are immediately put to a cruel death along with the adulterer.

This aforementioned king keeps his subjects under tight control and is terribly feared.[1]

He has tremendous income, with houses full of elephant's tusks, some of them full of copper, and many of them with *lebongos*, which are common currency here and are made from grass and are woven by the natives.

This king has over 500 children by his concubines, but all these children are of little status. The sons are mostly thieves and the daughters whores. Also, these children cannot come to the crown, but his sister's children can. They say they know that the children from the sister's side are royalty and that the king's children are not.[2]

When this kings drinks, no one can watch him, or else forfeit his neck. When he wants to drink a little bell is rung.[3] Then everyone around him falls on their faces. After he has drunk, it is rung again. Then everyone rises once again.[4]

During my time there, I saw that he continually spent his time with a young child who was his nephew, his own sister's son, and whom he kept with him and loved very much. This aforementioned child touched the king's arm by accident as he drank, and so he had this child immediately put to death, and had his blood brushed onto

[1] For an ethnography of royal power in modern Loango, see Hagenbucher-Sacripanti, *Les Fondements spirituels du pouvoir au royaume de Loango*.

[2] Van den Broecke's description of matrilineality in Loango royal succession corroborates the accounts of Battel (Ravenstein, *Strange Adventures*, p. 50) and Van Wassenaer (*Historisch verhael*, October 1624: f. 27r). Brun observed that patrilineal succession, to the king's first born son, was preferred, but otherwise the throne went to king's sister's son (Jones, *German Sources*, p. 50). Royal succession in Loango was no doubt as contentious as the abrupt transfer of power in any other society, hence the succession probably had 'both elective and hereditary features' (Martin, *External Trade of the Loango Coast*, p. 25).

[3] Unfortunately, Van den Broecke gave no indication whether this bell, so symbolic of kingship in Central Africa, was of the single or double flange-welded clapperless type. See Vansina, 'The Bells of Kings'.

[4] The content of this paragraph is similar to the reports of Battel (Ravenstein, *Strange Adventures*, p. 46) and Brun (Jones, *German Sources*, p. 56), and the description of Van Wassenaer (*Historisch verhael*, October 1624, f. 27v).

his idols and charms.[1] When I asked him why he was so cruel to his own kin and to an innocent child, he answered that it was better the child than himself, because (as the Devil had suggested to him) if he had not immediately had him [the child] put to death, than he himself would have to die.[2]

The king himself is a great magician and speaks often with the Devil. He knew long before my arrival that I was coming, and precisely on which day I would come to anchor in the bay, and also that I would bring him such and such goods, all of which was correct.[3]

The father of this king is still alive and is said to be 160 years old. He has never been king. If he now outlives this king, then his sixth son will also become king, who is now more than thirty-six years old. This old man is named Manni Goy, is blind, and had so little strength that he could not lift the weight of a Dutch lb off of the table. The king has some holidays, on which he presents himself outside of his palace on a raised tomb which the natives decorated in a nice and curious manner. Around him sit his principal nobles, and on the other side stood a few music (as they know it) players who play very melodiously on curved horns made from large and small elephant's tusks; upon which [time] the majority of nobles, one from each state, present themselves very triumphantly, according to rank, with all of their slaves. After many strange leaps and bounds[4] they end up lying on their bellies before the king, in submission until he orders them to rise.

The majority of their possessions is comprised of slaves, women, and children.

The people are pitch black all over, finely proportioned in body

[1] These 'idols' and 'charms' were probably the Kongo *miniski* (sing., *nkisi*), visual representations of spiritual personhood and power (MacGaffey and Harris, *Astonishment and Power*, pp. 21–103).

[2] The same story was recorded by Brun, who like Van den Broecke claimed to have personally witnessed the episode; he described the boy as nine years old, and as the king's own son (Jones, *German Sources*, pp. 56–7). Battell reported the same event (but did not claim to have witnessed it), and described the boy as twelve years old, and as the king's son (Ravenstein, *Strange Adventures*, pp. 45–6).

[3] For more on the *mani* Loango's prescience, see the Introduction, pp. 15–16.

[4] What seemed like bad choreography to Van den Broecke was a mimicry of the most important form of self-defence on the battlefield – leaping to avoid projectiles (see Thornton, 'The Art of War in Angola', pp. 363–4).

and limb with very well-shaped faces, good-natured, more loyal to our nation than to the Portuguese (who have frequented there for over forty years). They are not thievish, but instead hate very much those who are. They are most courteous and polite. When they meet each other they clap their hands and call 'sacarilla saccarilla', which is to say 'welcome'.[1]

The female population here is, on the average, lovelier than any other place in all of Africa. They are attentive their dress, which are just *labongos* made of grass and are about a square ell in size, which they wear on their right side[2] and which just covers their nakedness, front and back. They have their hair cut with a razor and smear their heads with oil from the coconut-palm and smear their entire bodies with red paint made from stone-ground *taccola*. These women always go with a mat under their arms on which to sit when they go somewhere for a chat. Many have good numbers of beads, which they know how to make themselves from shells, and which are held in great esteem.

The men wear on their heads caps made of grass, very pretty and neatly stitched with a needle, some of which are decorated with feathers of different colours. Their clothes are also made of grass and bound like a skirt, which they tie around their middle with a quarter ell of cloth, but more often with bark from trees, so that their bodies are usually covered from their hips down and above that they are naked. On top of that, decorative skins from exotic animals, such as leopards, monkeys, civet cats, and others, hang in front of their bellies. Also [they wear] many copper and silver arm-rings, and most of them have buffalo-tails over their shoulders, to shoo away flies off their naked upper bodies as needed.

Each man has as many wives as he can feed.[3] The men keep them under terrible constraint, but the ordinary man has to make do with only one wife.

[1] Brun translated the greeting 'Sacarella, Sacarella' to mean 'we are glad, we are glad you have come.' Jones suggested it may be a Kikongo greeting, '*sakalala*', meaning 'to be or become well ... to be full of joy' (Jones, *German Sources*, p. 49, with n. 24).

[2] That is, hang on their right shoulder.

[3] See also Van Wassenaer (*Historisch verhael*, October 1624: f. 27v): 'The man marries as many women as he wants'.

The wives must provide a living for the man by seeding, planting, working the land with hoes,[1] and doing much other, very hard labour. Meanwhile the man lies idly on his side (more or less like the lazy women in Spain). When the man wants to eat, the wife must stand and serve him until he is finished eating, bring him water for his hands, and then leaves with the scraps to eat alone in the kitchen. Their diet is mostly *bannannus* [= plantains], *batatas* [= sweet potatoes], pineapples, beans, and beautiful large peas.[2] The bread [= ?porridge] is made from *mili* [= maize] dough. Besides that they have much fish, elephant-meat, chickens, capons, *cabriten*,[3] buffalo and other wild animals as well. They use much palm oil in their food. The drink is water, palm wine and *thombo*.[4] Many use, throughout the day, a certain fruit named *colla*.[5] It is bitter when chewed, then after the sap is spit out it becomes increasingly sweet. In its use it is similar to the *siri pinnan* of the Indies.[6] Some cannot live without this *colla* (which here is called *casso*)[7]. Finally, some can fast on it for the entire day, and they say it is very good for your stomach, as I myself found through experience.

Everyone must guard himself in these areas from going off with the women or associating with them too much, because there is not a single one [man] in ten who will escape getting a terrible sickness, and die on the ninth day after falling ill, because their nature does not agree with ours, as I myself found during my stay of roughly sixteen months ashore. If someone of our nation falls sick after having been with these women many times, he should take care not to let himself be bled or else he will without a doubt die, because there is not one

[1] See also Van Wassenaer (ibid., October 1624: f. 27v): 'The women cultivate the land'.

[2] These 'peas' are identified later in this 'Description' as groundnuts.

[3] Van den Broecke used the Portuguese word for goat, *cabrito*. Dutch travellers typically used this word for both goats and African hair sheep, which they perhaps mistook for goats.

[4] Brun described *matumba* as a type of palm wine, albeit inferior, perhaps made from the raffia palm rather than the preferred oil palm type (Jones, *German Sources*, p. 54, with n. 53). Van Wassenaer (*Historisch verhael*, October 1624: f. 26v) made exactly the same distinction, referring to this inferior wine as *thombo*.

[5] The kola nut (*Cola nitida*).

[6] In south-east Asia the leaves and nut of the betel palm (*Areca catechu*) are chewed as a stimulant.

[7] Kikongo, *nkasu*

in a hundred who shall survive. So dangerous is it here to pick up these *luckxsuriusse*[1] women.[2] These aforementioned women are so strong in nature that on the day before giving birth to children, they still stand and work the land with a young child strapped on their back, and in sum doing other, heavier labour. And more amazing than anything else, is that right after they have given birth they go into the water with the child and all, to wash themselves. Some of them will not wait two days before going off to bed with the man, but a few of quality wait a month or more.[3]

As for their religion, there is not much to write. Some believe in Mahomet,[4] others are heathens and worship the moon and others the sun, but for the most part it is the Devil in whom they have found a strange comfort. When asked why they worship the Devil, and not our Saviour Jesus Christ, they answer that they do not know him, but do indeed know the Devil well, whom they see and speak with regularly. So it is a terrible thing that these people are still so blind.

They believe firmly that when one of them dies they rise again and become as white as we are. They are buried with their most important treasures and jewels around them, and above, at the head, is placed each morning and evening a pot of palm wine with some food, to drink while under way. They continue to do so for a year or two with weeping and wailing like a dog.[5]

They are no warriors, in spite of the fact that they have many arms. I was ashore there for more than thirty months and never did I

[1] See entry for 29 March 1608, with annotation.

[2] Van den Broecke's identification of the 'nature' of African women as the cause of their European sexual partners' sickness is certainly mistaken, nor would any venereal disease kill its victims so quickly. But European men who spent any time at all onshore were in risk of contracting endemic diseases (like malaria) and infections (such as dysentery) which could result in their rapid death.

[3] Compare with Van den Broecke's description of women's work, delivering babies, and washing in his 'Manners and Customs of Cape Verde', above, p. 38.

[4] Van den Broecke's report of Muslims in Central Africa at this time is certainly incorrect. It is possible that he simply confused his notes for Senegambia, where he described Islam as a popular faith (above, p. 36), when composing this description of Loango.

[5] *Karmen gelijck een hoffhondt* could also be translated as the English colloquialism, 'howling like a wolf'.

see them injure or draw blood from one another. When one becomes angry at another, they wrestle against each other, and do so until one has the other under his foot [= at his mercy]. During my stay, I had a fit of rage and hit the boy [= ?houseboy], who started to bleed, at which the women and some men started wailing, from which I sensed that they are a compassionate and caring people.

The natives are very good fishermen and catch great numbers of fish. There, in the morning, sometimes more than 300 manned canoes go out to sea, and return to land at midday at the height of the sun.

Saw a man in Loango who was nine Dutch feet tall

The first time I came ashore at Loango, I saw a black native of this country who was nine Dutch feet tall and was well proportioned accordingly. This man's father, who stood nearby, was not more than four and a half feet tall and his brother, who was born close [in time] to him, was around thirty years old and just three of my [Dutch] feet tall. Many people of this country worshipped this man because of his height.

Many elephant's tusks are found here. During my stay, more than 50,000 lb were traded each year, of which I exchanged more than 30,000 lb. There is also much beautiful red copper, most of which comes from the kingdom of the Insiques (who are at war with Loango) in the form of large copper arm-rings weighing between 1½ and 14 lb, [and are] smuggled out of the country.[1] Learned also that there lie silver, tin, and copper mines inland which are not being worked because the people are so lazy and are not accustomed to labour. Also found here in abundance are sugar cane and Benin pepper,[2] and beautiful ginger, furthermore other *mantimentos* or *viveres*[3] *such as* bannannissen [= plantains], pineapples, *patatis* [= sweet potatoes], *bachovus* [= bananas], yams, *masseffes*,[4] Turkish beans, and

[1] 'Insiques' refers to the Tio kingdom, whose king had the title *Anziko* (cf. p. 90 n.1 above). Martin argued that the Vili of Loango organized caravans into the interior to obtain copper from Mindouli (Martin, *External Trade of the Loango Coast*, pp. 36, 41–2). Van den Broecke's reference to the smuggling of copper, however, suggests continued Tio control over the metal-bearing valley.

[2] Benin pepper (*Piper guineense*).

[3] Van den Broecke gives two Portuguese synomyms for food: *manimentos* and *viveres*.

[4] This fruit is difficult to identify. Perhaps it was the safu plum (*Dacryodes edulis*), which Van den Broecke recorded with both a Bantu sixth class plural

tarwe milli,[1] large peas known here as *ingobos*,[2] lemons, *arang*-apples [= oranges[3]] also the fruit *colla,* which has already been mentioned in detail, scores of palm trees which are very popular with the natives because of the wine, which is their principal drink. Furthermore the oil which comes from them is very medicinal, and they cook with it. With the leaves[4] they cover their houses, which works very nicely. Well, they have many uses for these palm trees and without them they would be ...[5]

Furthermore there are animals and birds in abundance, such as great numbers of elephants, buffalos, oxen, sheep, goats, pigs, leopards, tigers, civet cats, all kinds of monkeys, hart, hind and other wild animals as well. Extremely beautiful pelts are found here. In this land there are also small horses which have such beautiful colours, like peacock's tails.[6] In the year 1596 the Portuguese sent three from Loanda de Ste Pauwel [= Luanda] via Bresiel [= Brazil] to the king as a present, but only two arrived safely.[7]

Salvagien along the Cacongo river

Around the river Cacongo, lying at the latitude of 5 degrees, is found a certain type of man that the Portuguese call *Salvagis*.[8] They are totally wild, cannot speak, walk naked, and have very shaggy hair over their entire body. On the back above the crack of the ass is a tail, similar in size to a thumb.[9] During my time there, I sent the junior merchant, Jan Janssen van der Graff, there to trade for tusks, and he saw one there, which had been shot with an arrow.

---

prefix (ma-) and a Dutch plural suffix (-s)? For the safu plum, see Vansina, *Paths in the Rainforests*, p. 287 n. 49.

[1] Literally, 'wheat *milli*'. Perhaps the 'wheat' refers to the open panicle of sorghum.

[2] *Kikongo jinguba* are American peanuts (*Arachis hypogaea*).

[3] Literally, 'orange apples', and similar to the Portuguese word for the fruit, *laranja*.

[4] Though Van den Broecke writes *bladers* ('leaves'), the composite leaves of the palm are usually designated 'fronds'.

[5] This sentence is incomplete in the original manuscript.

[6] Zebra. Compare with Battel's description (Ravenstein, *Strange Adventures*, p. 63).

[7] *Maer twee van in salvemento sijn gecomen*. *Salvamento* is a Portuguese word meaning 'safely'. The source of Van den Broecke's information about this has not been identified.

[8] Portuguese *selvaginos*, 'gorillas'.

[9] Cf. Battel's description (Ravenstein, *Strange Adventures*, p. 54).

The following are also found here in abundance: chickens, similar to the big ones from Lombardyen [= Lombardy, northern Italy], forty of which I purchased for a *reael van achten*. Furthermore there are very large parrots, wild geese, ducks, field-fowl, partridges, peacocks, quails, and other delicious birds as well.

Note: that I once satisfied my hunger, out of curiosity, with the tongues of grey parrots, and when I came home I sold a young one of these for thirty guilders in cash.

The Portuguese of Loanda de Ste Pauwel [=Luanda] have frequented here for over forty years. Their principal trade has been elephant's tusks, which buy they in lots of 120 Holland lb, or a *quintal,* for four ells of *palmilio* (blue cloth purchased in Portugal for only four *real* per ell). They also do a strong business in the local cloth known as *labongos,* which are used as money in Loando de St Pauvel [= Luanda], just the same as our money here [in Europe]. The soldiers of the king of Spain are paid with them in the *conquista* of Masagan [= Massangano], around thirty miles inland from Loando de Ste. Pauwel [=Luanda]. They purchase *taccola* in abundance and transport it along the entire coast, where it brings great profits.

This is as much as I have understood and seen in three voyages [to Loango] and during the roughly thirty months that I stayed ashore there.

On this 30th of October, 1612.

APPENDICES

APPENDIX A

WEIGHTS, MEASURES AND CURRENCY

Conversions to precise modern units are offered here merely as a rough guide for estimation rather than a definitive accounting which would warrant sophisticated supporting statistical analysis. Most weights, measures, and rates of exchange varied both within Europe and on the African coast.

1 Dutch lb (sing. *pond*, pl. *ponden*) = 490 grams
1 last = 4000 *ponden* (Amsterdam) = 1,976 kilograms
1 ell = .688 meter (Amsterdam)
1 *côvado* (Portuguese) = 3 *palmos* = 25.86 English inches = 65.7 centimetres
1 *quintal* (Portuguese) = 120 *ponden* = 36 kilograms
1 *voet* ('foot', pl. *voeten*) = 28.3 centimetres
1 *span* = 20 centimetres
1 land mile = 3 meridian minutes at 45 degrees latitude = 3.45 miles = 5. 56 kilometres
1 sea mile = 1 meridian minute at 45 degrees latitude = 1.15 miles =1.85 kilometres
1 *vadem* ('fathom') = 6 *voeten* = 1.7 metres
1 *vinger* ('finger') = 1/11 *voet* = 2.6 centimetres
1 *mengel* (liquid) = 1.2 litres
1 guilder (fl.) = 20 stuivers = 320 pennings
1 *peça* (Portuguese) = 6.15 grams of gold = 8 guilders
1 *benda* (gold) = 61 grams = 2 Troy ounces
4 *réis* = 2.10 guilders

APPENDIX B

EARLIER EDITIONS OF THE VAN DEN BROECKE MANUSCRIPT

As indicated in the Introduction, I strongly suspect that the manuscript preserved in the library of University of Leiden is a re-working of some other notes or documents that Van Broecke kept contemporaneous to his trips abroad. What follows is a tentative (and certainly incomplete) list of publications that cite Pieter van den Broecke as an author of material relating to Africa. I have provided some brief comments only on those works with which I am currently familiar. Unfortunately these represent only a few of the total, and thus a complete 'genealogy' detailing the historical interaction of these texts is, at the moment, impossible for me to reconstruct. This list is arranged in chronological order. For the earliest editions, the printer's name is given as the publisher.[1]

1. *Korte Historiael ende Journaelsche Aenteyckeninghe, Van al 't gheen merck-waerdich voorgevallen is, in de langhduerighe Reysen, soo nae Cabo Verde, Angola, &c. als insonderheydt van Oost-Indien; beneffens de bescrijvingh en af-beeldingh van verscheyden Steden, op de Custe van Indien, Persien, Arabien, en aen 't Roode Meyr: Aldereerst (van wegen de Ghecotroyeerde Oost-Indische Compaignie) besocht, en opghedaen, Door Pieter van den Broecke.* Haarlem: Hans Passchiers van Wesbusch, 1634.

This is a heavily edited version of Van den Broecke's manuscript. A full two-thirds of its African letters have been excised. Much of the remaining text has been changed and re-worked. These passages are conspicuous by the use of spellings and vocabulary that are at odds with Van den

[1] I located all of the 17th-century and most of the 18th-century editions in John Lanwehr, *VOC: A Bibliography of Publications Relating to the Dutch East India Company, 1602–1800* (Utrecht, 1991). The other editions I traced through a myriad of footnotes, or stumbled upon by pure luck.

Broecke's usage, as evidenced in his manuscript. The editing may have been aimed at polishing Van den Broecke's image. For example, his criticism in the manuscript of Wemmer van Barchum's insolence was removed, and sexually suggestive passages were re-worked (in spelling not his own) to suggest that he spurned the advances of the *mani* Loango's sister. This edition also includes other information not in the manuscript: Van den Broecke's dedication of the book to the *bewindhebbers* of the VOC; two poems praising the author; an engraved frontispiece; and an introduction which claims that Van den Broecke's voyages to Africa were undertaken while he was employed 'by Elias Trip and thereafter by Jacques Niquet'. This edition includes several drawings not part of the original manuscript; in the African 'letters', these are the four drawings of fish and the image of hippopotamuses. The text is set in Roman and Italic type.

2. [same title as #1] Amsterdam: Joost Boersz, 1634.

Apparently a re-setting of the Haarlem edition with minor changes in spelling and grammar. This text is set in semi-gothic bold block type, with Roman type used for emphasis. The copy which I inspected (at the University of Leiden) had no etching of Van den Broecke, nor those of fish and hippopotamuses which are found in the Haarlem edition.

3. 'Historische ende Iournaelsche aenteyckeningh, Van 't gene Pieter van den Broecke op sijne Reysen, soo van Cabo Verde, Angola,Guinea, en Oost-Indien (aenmercens waerdingh) voorghevallen is &c.' In Issac Commelin, *Begin ende Voortgangh Van De Vereenighde Nederlantsche Geoctroyeerde Oost-indische Compagnie* ..., Vol. II, chapter 15. Amsterdam: Jan Jansz, 1645.

4. 'Wonderlijcke Historische Ende Journaelsche Aenteyckeningh, Van 't ghene Pieter van den Broecke, Op sijne Reysen, soo van Cabo Verde, Angola, Gunea, Oost-Indien: Waer in hem, soo in Schip-breuck, als in 't door-reysen van 't Landt, seer veel vremde dinghen ontmoet sijn, soo van Religie, Manieren, Zeeden, en Huys-houdingen der volckeren: En andere eyghenschappen de Landen en Kusten die sy bezeylt hebben.' In Joost Hartgerts, *Oost-Indische Voyagie*..., Chapter 7. Amsterdam: Joost Hartgerts, 1648.

This is a copy of the Amsterdam edition (or #3?), minus illustrations, but after the entry for June 1607 there is an *inwerp* ('toss in') of a description of the 'Kingdom of Congo' written by an unidentified source. Text was set in semi-gothic bold block. The copy which I inspected had no illustrations in its African parts other than rather standard, Dutch block-prints of ships and block letter-images at the beginning of each chapter which cited Biblical readings.

5. 'Vijf verscheynde Journaelen Van Pieter van den Broeck,Gehouden op zijne Reysen, na Cabo-verde, Angola, Doch voornamentlijck na Oost-indien, Waer in hem, soo in Schip-breuck, als in 't door-reysen van 't Landt, seer veel vremde dinghen ontmoet zijn; Als mede van de Religie, Manieren, Zeeden, en Huys-houdingen der Volckeren, oock de eyghenschappen de Landen en Kusten die hy bezeylt heeft.' In Gillis Joosten Saeghman, *Verscheyde Oost-indische Voyagien...*, Vol. I, Chapter 13. Amsterdam: Gillis Joosten Saeghman, [ca. 1663–1670].

This edition draws its text from #2 (or #3 or #4?), but removes all of the 'thank God' portions as well as the honorific titles bestowed on the 'gentlemen' of Amsterdam.

6. 'Voiaghe De Pierre van den Broeck Au Cap Vert, A Angola, Et Aux Indes Orientales...'. In R. A. Constantin de Renneville, *Recueil des voyages qui ont servi a L'établissement et aus proges de la Compagnie des Indes Orientales ...*, Vol. III Chapter P. Amsterdam, 1702–6.

7. Ratelband, K.,ed., *Reizen naar West-Afrika van Pieter van den Broecke, 1605–1614.* 's-Gravenhage: Martinus Nijhoff, 1950.

Ratelband inherited the project of transcribing and annotating the University of Leiden manuscript for publication in the Linschoten-Vereeniging series from Professor J. C. M. Warnsinck, who died in 1943. Ratelband was not a trained academic, but rather a Dutch businessman with substantial trading interests and experience in Central Africa, and was a veteran of many trips to Luanda. This personal enthusiasm for the items, prices, and activities of trade is readily apparent in both his introduction and annotation. Though not a professional historian, he knew that archives were indeed a wonderful place to hide, and this is what he did during the Nazi occupation of the Netherlands.[1] To my knowledge, this is the first publication of the entire Leiden manuscript's

[1] Phyllis Martin, personal communication, 11 January 1994.

African sections. It is supplemented by illustrations taken from one of the 1634 books, a reproduction of Frans Hals's portrait of Van den Broecke, an engraving similar to the portrait, and illustrations of Loango from Olfert Dapper's *Naukeruige Beschrijvinghe der Afrikaensche Gewesten*. It includes a suggestive genealogy of Pieter de Marees which was included in neither the Naber nor the Van Dantzig and Jones editions of that work. The principal problem of using this edition for research nowadays is that it was published long ago, before the emergence of modern academic African history and the more recent attention given within the sub-field to using early European-language sources for early African history.

8. Cuvelier, Jean, ed., 'L'Ancien Congo d'après Pierre van den Broecke (1608–12).' *Bulletin des séances de l'Académie royale des sciences coloniales*, 1, 2, 1955, pp. 168–92.

9. 'Voyage of Pierre van den Broeck to Cape Verde, 1606.' In Elizabeth Donnan, ed., *Documents Illustrative of the History of the Slave Trade to America*. Washington, 1932; reprinted New York: Octagon Books, 1969. Vol. I, pp. 122–3.

This is a jumble of short extracts in French from Renneville (#6), with very sparse, very poor annotation.

10. Thilmans, Guy, and de Moraes, Nize Izabel, eds, 'Les Passages à la Petite Côte de Pieter van den Broecke (1606–1609).' *Bulletin de l'Institut fondamental de l'Afrique noire*, sér. B., 39, 3 (1977), pp. 471–92.

This is a generally reliable French translation of Ratelband's transcription and annotation of Van den Broecke's first voyage to Cape Verde and of excerpts dealing with Cape Verde taken from Van den Broecke's later voyages. It includes a summary, in French, of Ratelband's introduction, and a few additional notes on the area.

APPENDIX C

MAPS

Map 1: Voyage to Cape Verde

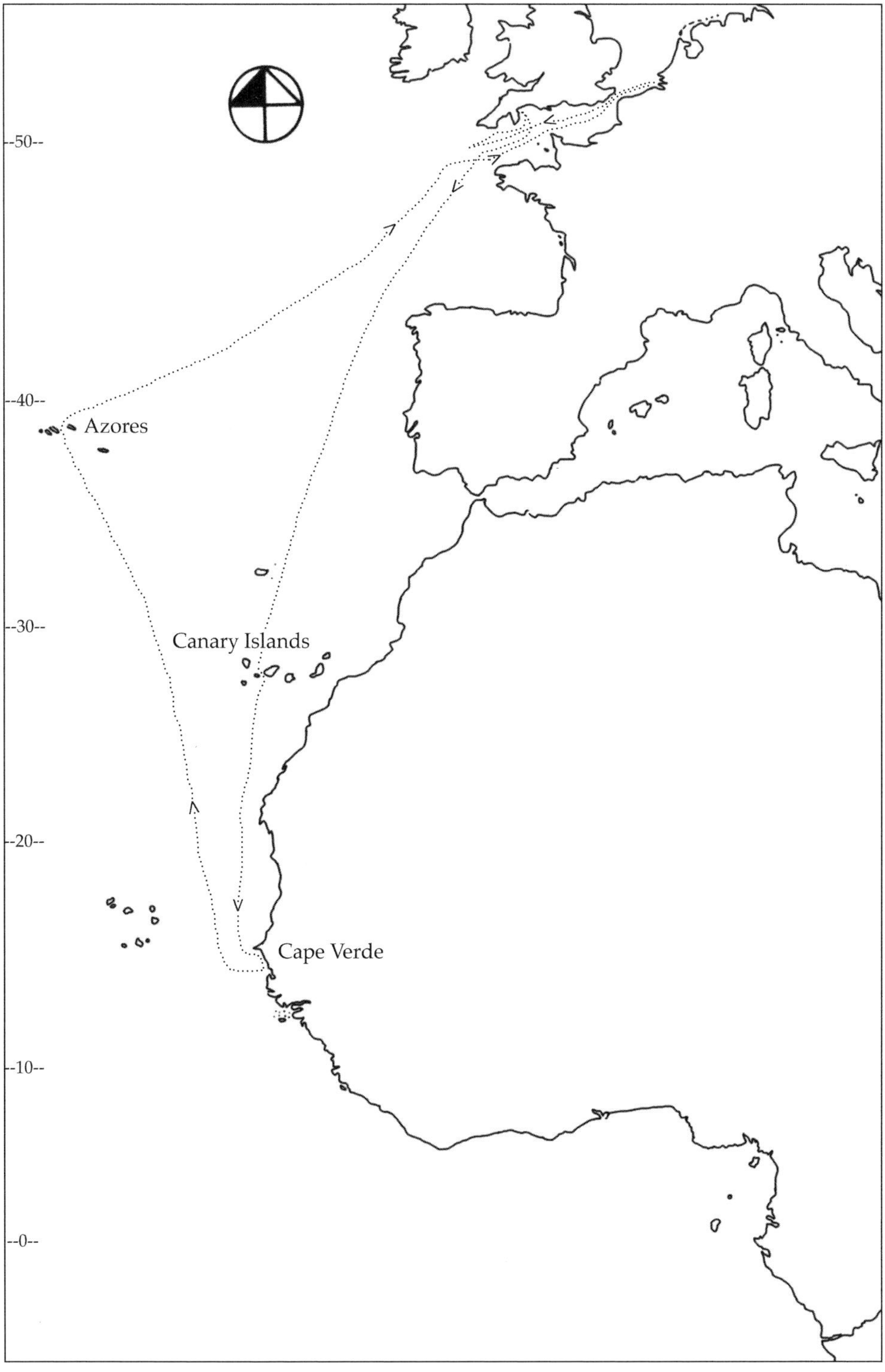

Map 2: First Voyage to 'Angola'

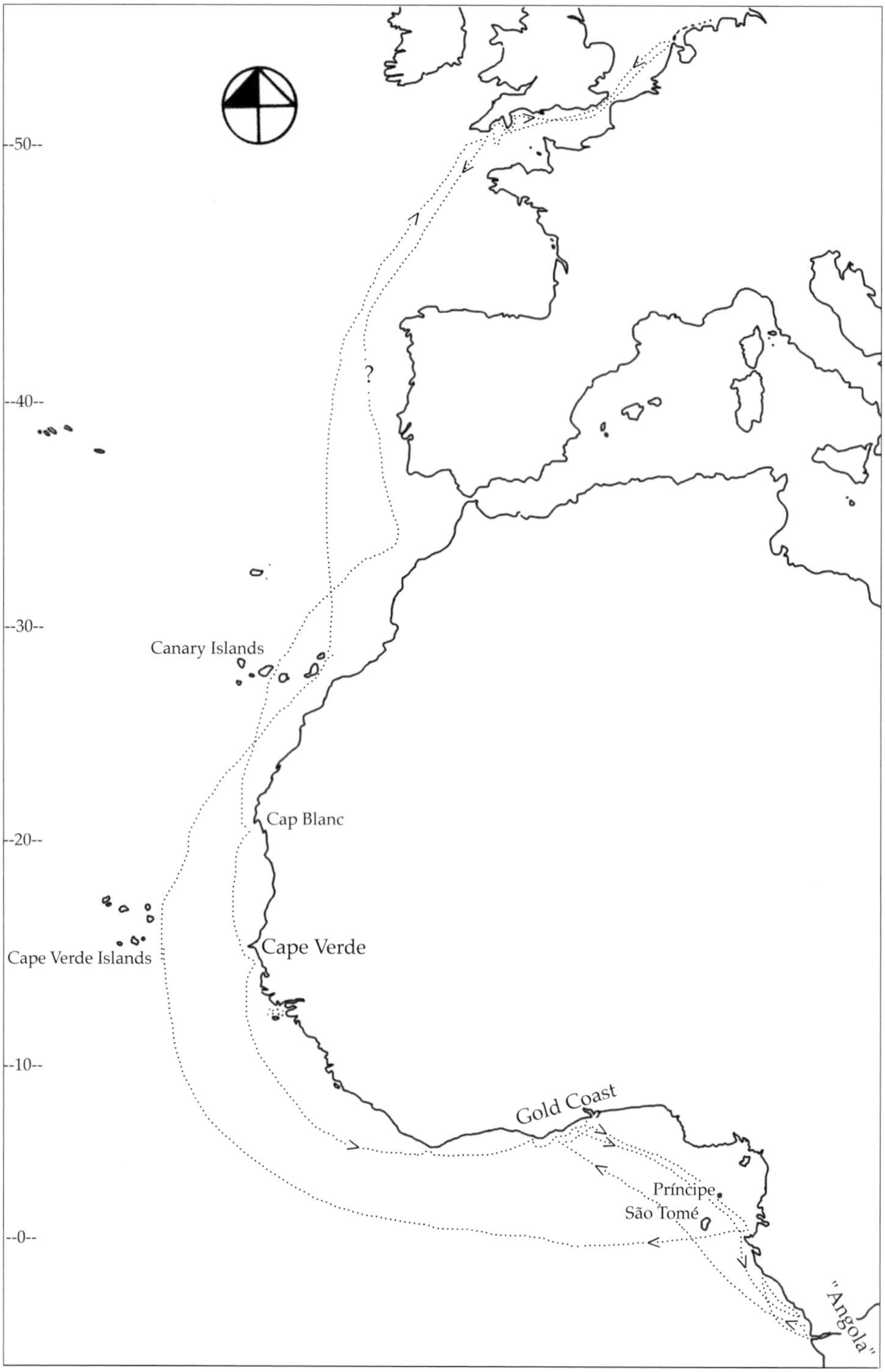

Map 3: Second Voyage to 'Angola'

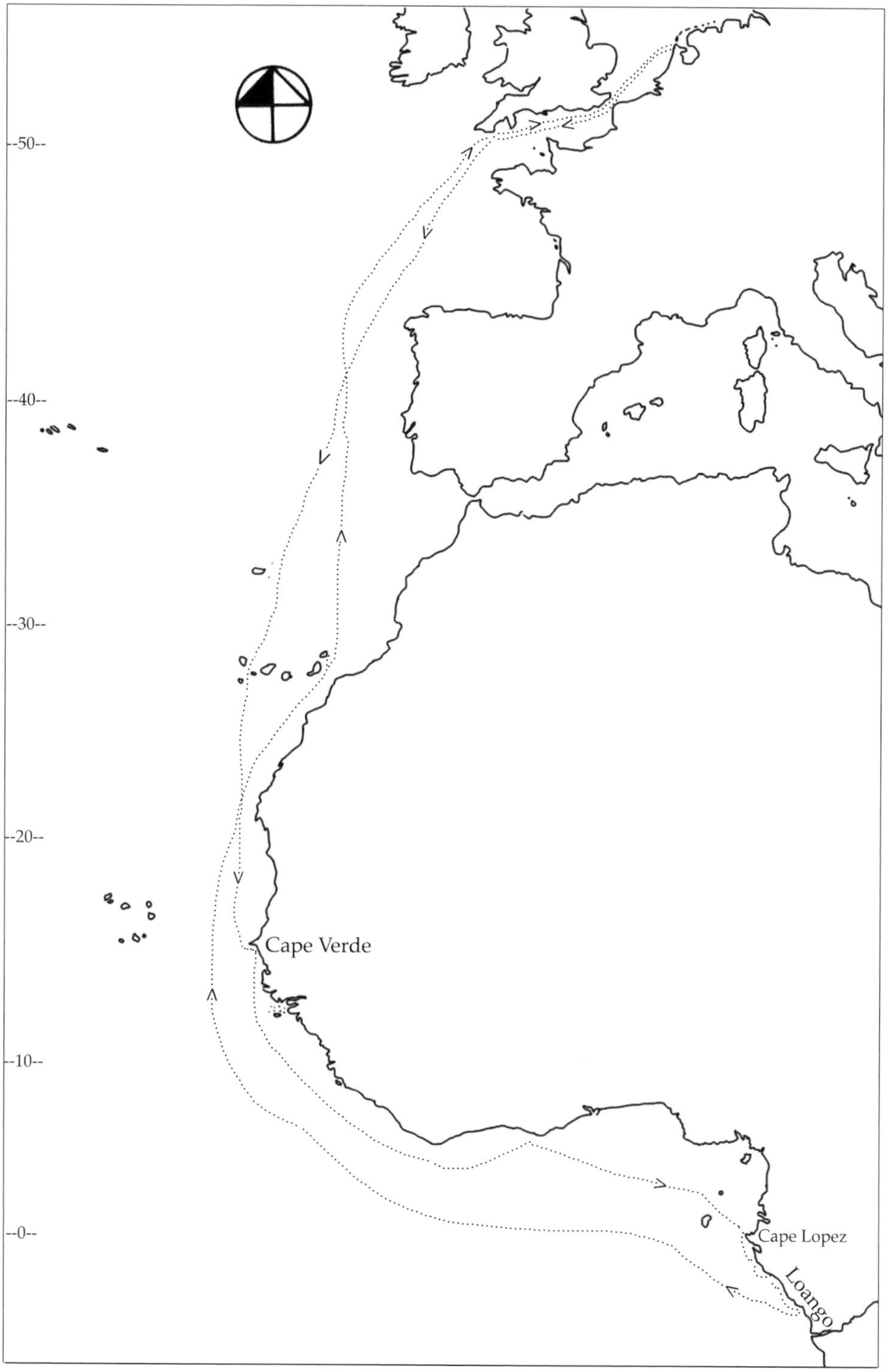

Map 4: Third Voyage to 'Angola'

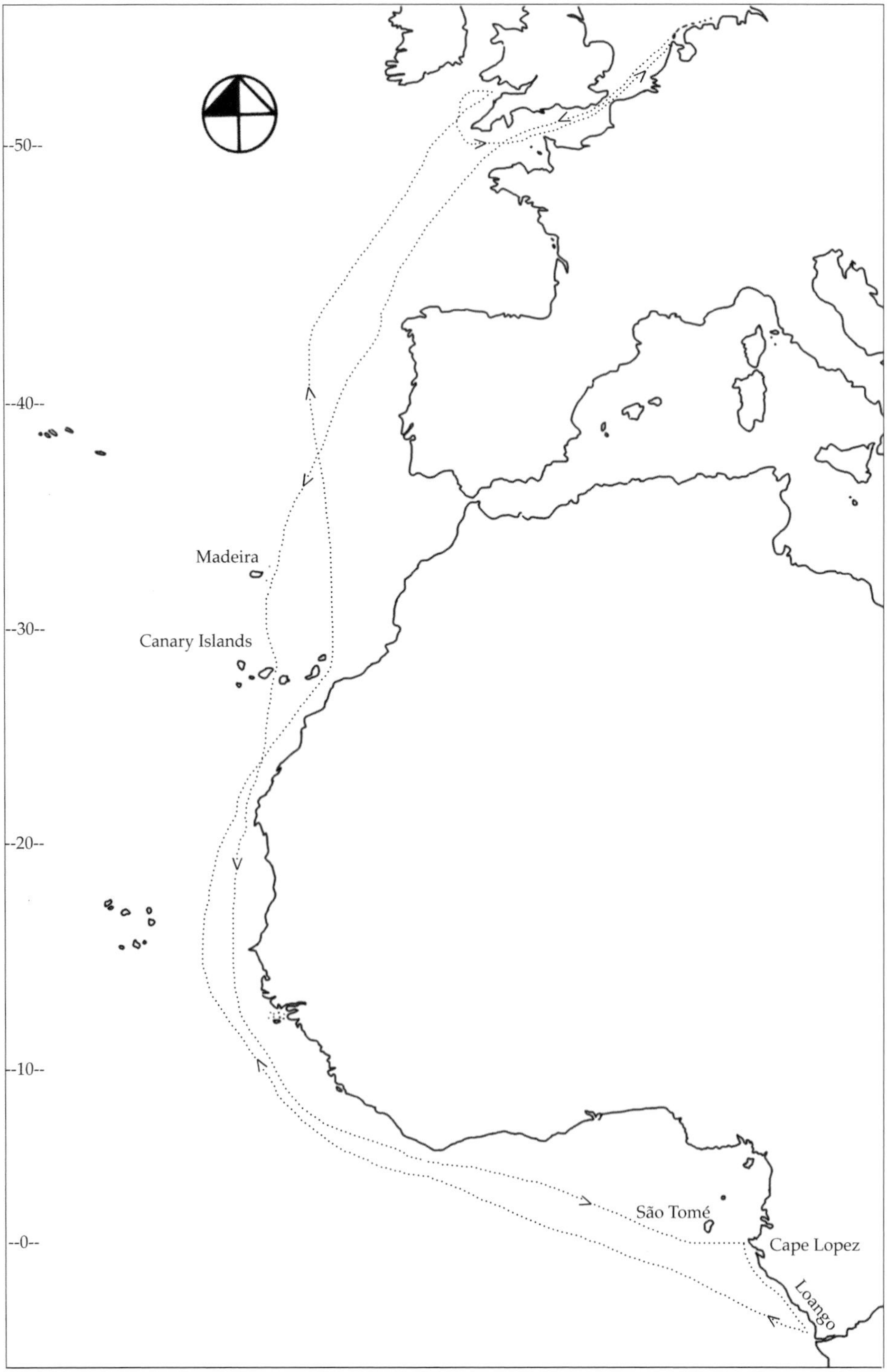

Map 5: Loango and 'Angola'

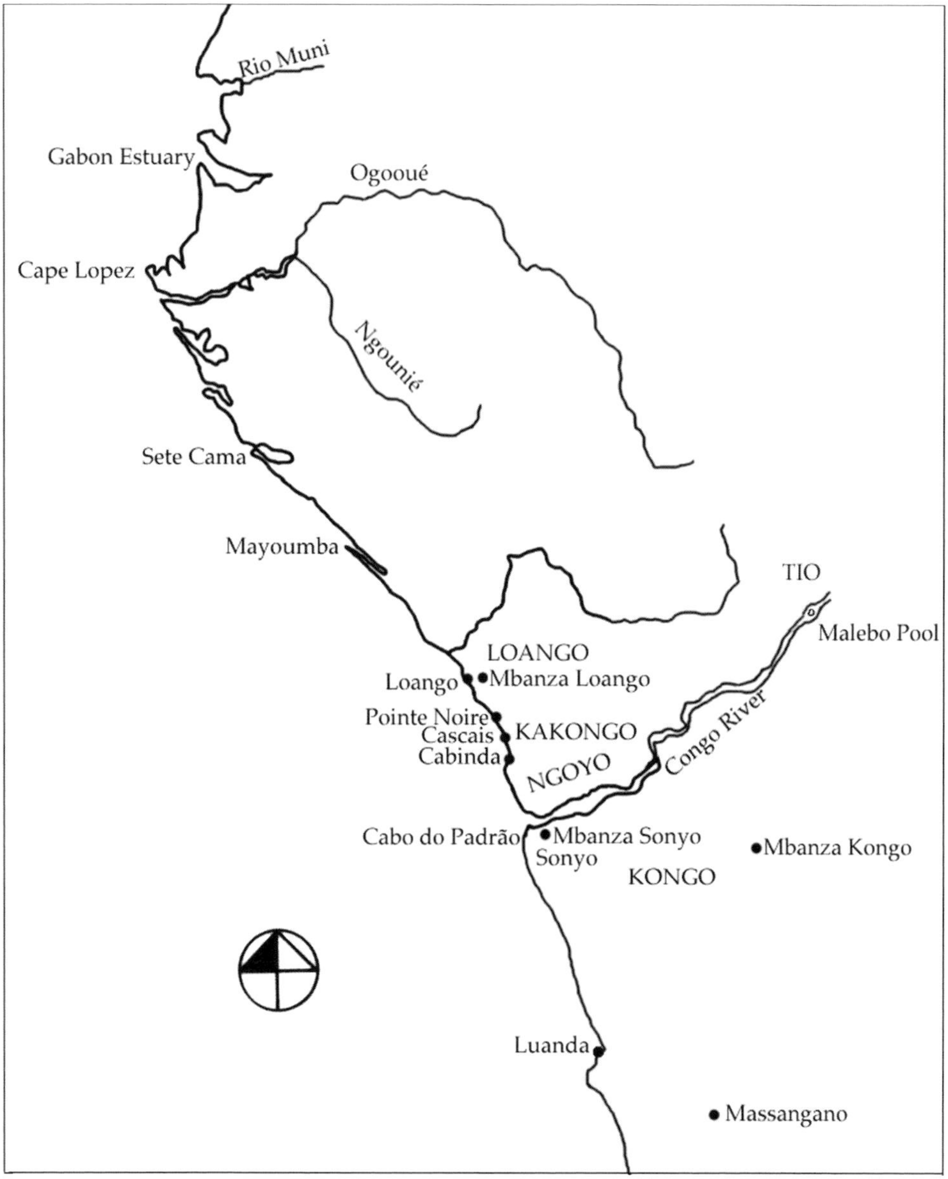

Map 6: Cape Verde

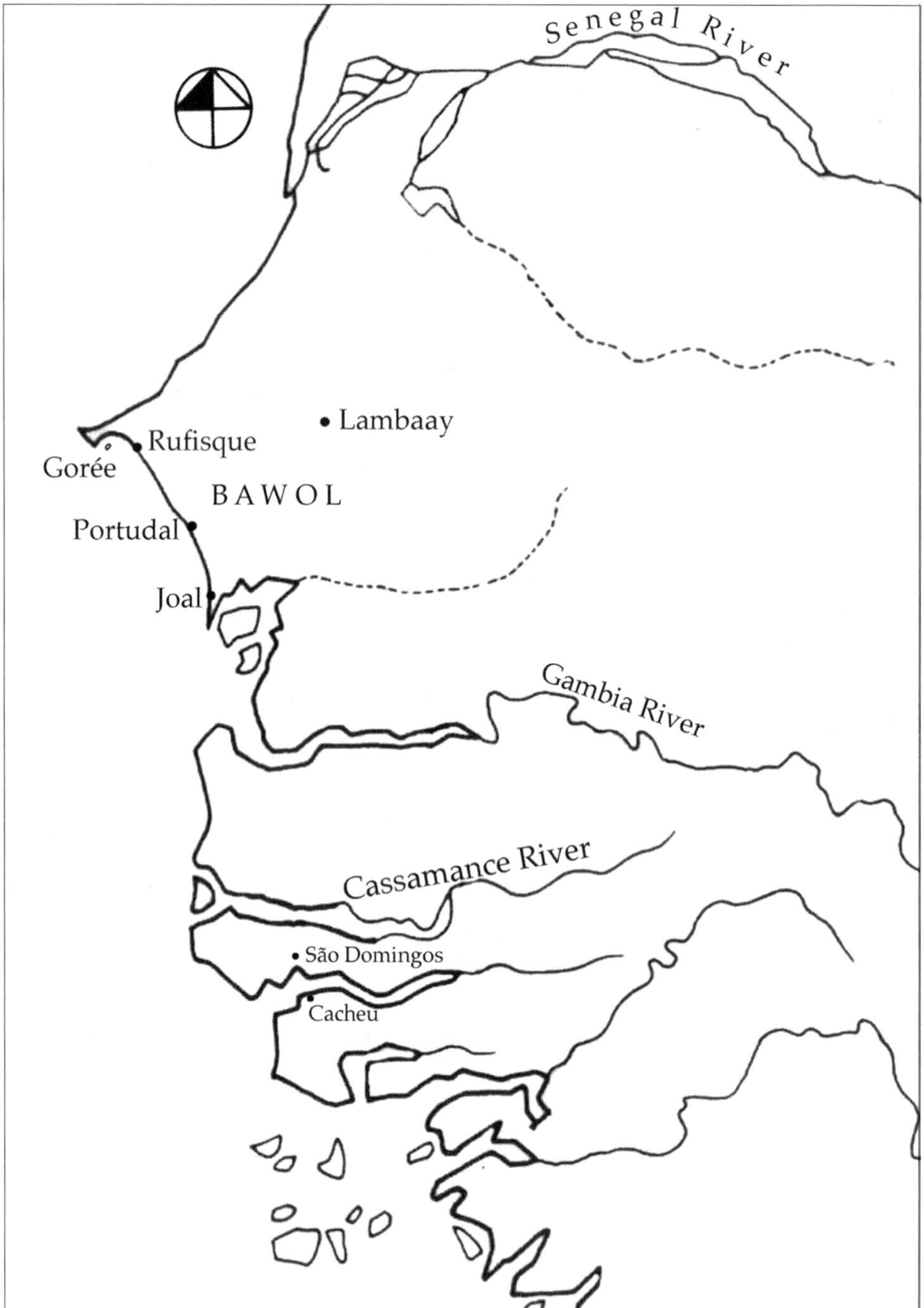

Map 7: The Gold Coast

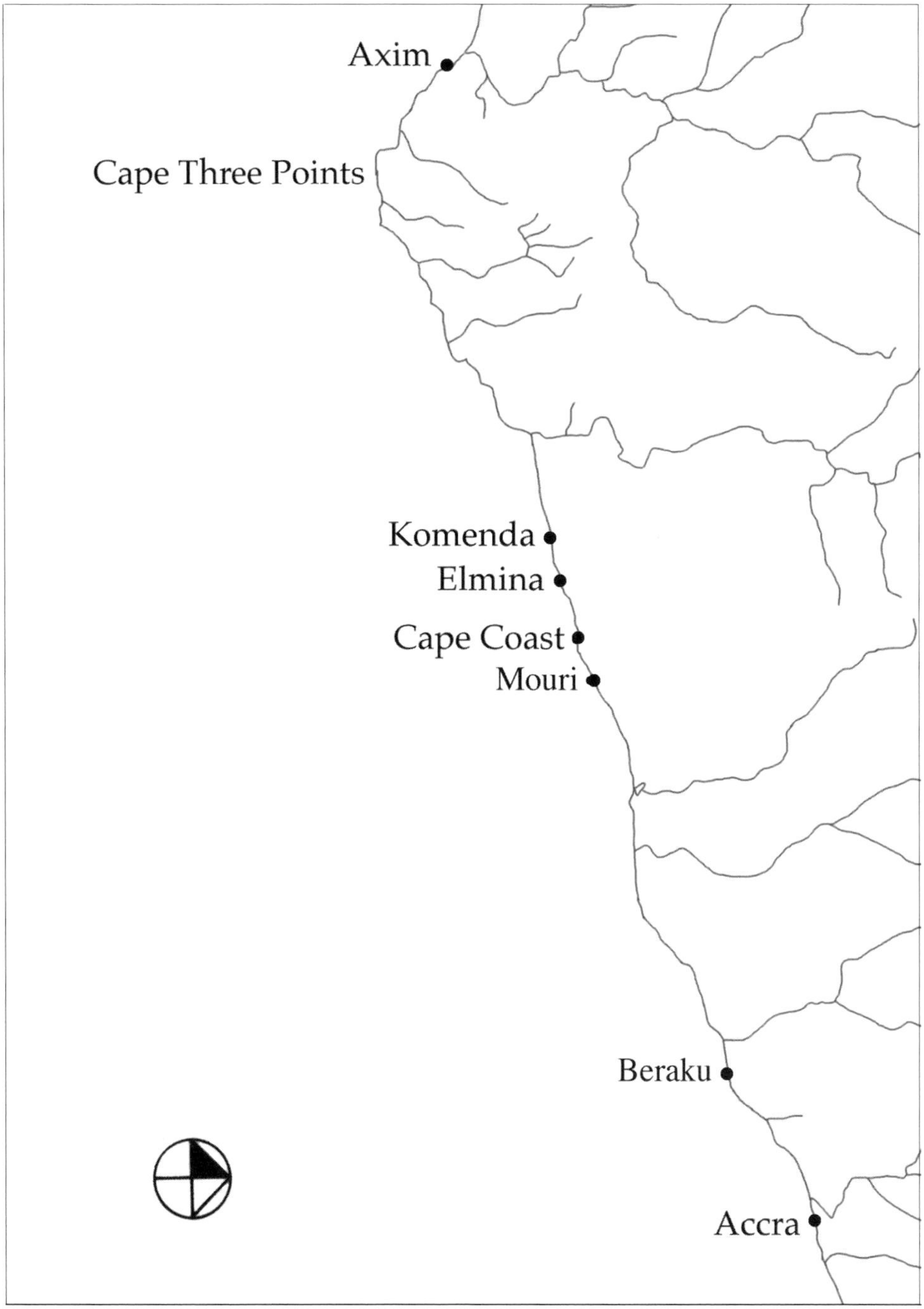

BIBLIOGRAPHY OF WORKS CITED

Alexis de Saint-Lô. See Thilmans and De Moraes, 1974.

Alvares de Almada, André. See Hair, 1984.

Alpern, Stanley B., 'The Introduction of Crops into West Africa in Precolonial Times', *History In Africa*, 19, 1992, pp. 13–43.

Asaert, Gustaaf, *et al.*, *Maritieme Geschiedenis der Nederlanden*, 3 vols, Bussum, 1977.

Barbot, Jean. See Hair, Jones, and Law, 1992

Battel, Andrew. See Ravenstein, 1967

Becker, Charles, 'Notes sur les conditions écologiques en Sénégambie aux 17e et 18e siècles', *African Economic History*, 14, 1985, pp. 167–211.

Birmingham, David, *Trade and Conflict in Angola: The Mbundu and their Neighbours Under the Influence of the Portuguese, 1483–1790*, Oxford, 1966.

Bittremieux, Leo, *Mayombish Idioticon*, 2 vols, Ghent, 1922.

Blake, J. W., *Europeans in West Africa, 1450–1560*, London, Hakluyt Society, 2nd series, 1942; reprinted Nendelen, 1967.

Blench, Roger, 'Prehistory of African Ruminant Livestock, Horses and Ponies', in Thurstan Shaw, Paul Sinclier, Bassey Andah and Alex Opoko, eds, *The Archaeology of Africa: Food, Metals and Towns*, London & New York, 1993, pp. 71–103.

Blussé, L. and Gaastra, F., eds, *Companies and Trade: Essays on Overseas Trading Companies during the Ancien Régime,* Leiden, 1981.

Boulègue, Jean, *Le Grand Jolof (XIIIe–XVIe siècle)*, Paris, 1987.

——, *Les Luso-Africains de Sénégambie*. Lisbon, Ministério da Educação, 1989.

Boxer, C. R., *The Dutch Seaborne Empire: 1600–1800*. New York, 1965.

Brásio, A., *Monumenta missionaria africana: Africa ocidental (1600–1622)*, sér. 2, IV, Lisbon, Agência Geral do Ultramar, Divisão de Publicações e Biblioteca, 1968.

Braudel, Fernand, *The Wheels of Commerce,* New York, 1979.

Brooks, George, *Landlords and Strangers: Ecology, Society and Trade in Western Africa, 1000–1630*, Boulder, Colorado, 1993.

Brouwer, C. G., 'Le Voyage au Yémen de Pieter van den Broecke (serviteur de la V.O.C.) en 1620, d'après son livre résolutions', in I. A. El-Sheikh *et al.*, *The Challenge of the Middle East*, Amsterdam, 1982, pp. 1–11.

——, 'Under the Watchful Eye of Mimī Bin ʿAbd Allāh: The Voyage of the Dutch Merchant Pieter van den Broecke to the Court of Djaʿfar Bāshā in Sana'a, 1616', in Robert Ross and George Winius, eds, *All of One Company: The VOC in Biographical Perspective*, Utrecht, 1986, pp. 42–72.

Brulez, Wilfred, 'De Diaspora der Vlaamse kooplui op het einde der XVI eeuw', *Bijdragen voor Geschiedenis der Nederlanden*, 15, 1960, pp. 279–306.

Bruijn, Jaap R., *The Dutch Navy of the Seventeenth and Eighteenth Centuries*, Columbia, South Carolina, 1993.

Brun, Samuel. See Jones, 1983; Naber, 1913.

Bühnen, Stephen, 'Place Names as an Historical Source: An Introduction with Examples from Southern Senegambia and Germany', *History in Africa* 19, 1992, pp. 45–101.

Carreira, António, *Panaria Cabo-Verdiano-Guineense: Aspectos históricos e socio-económicos,* Lisbon, Junta de Investigaçôes do Ultramar, 1968.

Clark, Randall B., 'Black Gold: The Portuguese Slave Trade from Angola, 1575–1641, unpublished Distinguished Majors (BA) Thesis, University of Virginia, 1988.

Coolhaas, W. P., ed., *Pieter van den Broecke in Azië*, 2 vols, 's-Gravenhage, 1962–3.

Curtin, Philip D., *Economic Change in Precolonial Africa,* Madison, Wisconsin, 1975.

——, 'Africa in the Wider Monetary World, 1200–1850', in J. F. Richards, ed., *Precious Metals in the Later Medieval and Early Modern Worlds*, Durham, South Carolina, 1983, pp. 231–68.

Dapper, Olfert, *Naukeurige Beschrijvinge der Afrikaensche Gewesten*, 2nd ed., Amsterdam, 1676.

Davies, D. W., *A Primer of Dutch Seventeenth Century Overseas Trade*, The Hague, 1961.

De Marees, Pieter. See Naber 1912; Van Dantzig and Jones, 1987.

De Moraes, N. I., 'Le Commerce des peaux à la Petite Côte aux XVIIe siècle', *Notes africaines* 134, 1972, pp. 37–45.

Duncan, T. Bentley, *Atlantic Islands: Madeira, the Azores and the Cape Verdes in Seventeenth-Century Commerce and Navigation*, Chicago, 1972.

Elias, Johan E., *De Vroedschap van Amsterdam, 1578–1795*, 2 vols, Haarlem, 1903–5.

Elbl, Ivana, 'The Portuguese Trade with West Africa', unpublished PhD thesis, University of Toronto, 1986.

Fage, John, *A Guide to Original Sources for Precolonial Western Africa Published in European Languages*, Madison, African Studies Program, University of Wisconsin-Madison, 1994.

Feinberg, Harvey M. and Johnson, Marion, 'The West African Ivory Trade during the Eighteenth Century: The "... and Ivory" Complex', *International Journal of African Historical Studies*, 15, 3, 1982, pp. 435–53.

Gamble, David P., and P. E. H. Hair, *The Discovery of River Gambra (1623) by Richard Jobson*, London, Hakluyt Society, 3rd series, 1999.

Garrard, Timothy F., *Akan Weights and the Gold Trade*, London, 1980.

Gibson, Charles, 'Conquest and So-Called Conquest in Spain and Spanish America', *Terrae Incognitae*, 12, 1980, pp. 1–19.

Gibson, Gordon D. and Cecilia R. McGurk, 'High-Status Caps of the Kongo and Mbundu Peoples', *Textile Museum Journal*, 4, 4, 1977, pp. 71–96.

Green, Jeremy N., *The Loss of the VOC Retourschip Batavia, Western Australia 1629*, Oxford, 1989.

Grimm, Claus, *Frans Hals: the Complete Works*, New York, 1990.

Hagenbucher-Sacripanti, Frank, *Les Fondements spirituels de pouvoir au royaume de Loango*, Paris, 1973.

Hair, P. E. H. , trans. and ed., *André Alvares de Almada: Brief Treatise on the Rivers of Guinea*, Liverpool, Department of History, University of Liverpool, 1984.

——, *The Founding of the Castelo São Jorge da Mina: An Analysis of the Sources*, Madison, African Studies Program, University of Wisconsin-Madison, 1994.

——, 'Attitudes to Africans in English Primary Sources on Guinea up to 1650', *History in Africa* 26, 1999, pp. 43–68.

Hair, P. E. H., Adam Jones, and Robin Law, eds, *Barbot on Guinea: The Writings of Jean Barbot on West Africa, 1678–1712*, 2 vols, London, Hakluyt Society, 2nd series, 1992.

Hair, P. E. H., and Robin Law, 'The English in Western Africa to 1700', in William Roger Loius, ed., *Oxford History of the British Empire*, vol. I, Oxford, 1998, pp. 241–63.

Hemmersam, Michael. See Jones, 1983

Henige, David, 'The Race is Not Always to the Swift: Thoughts on the Use of

Written Sources for the Study of Early African History', *Paideuma*, 33, 1987, pp. 53–79.

Hernæs, Per, *Slaves, Danes, and African Coast Society: The Danish Slave Trade from West Africa and Afro-Danish Relations on the Eighteenth Century Gold Coast*, Trondheim, 1995.

Hilton, Anne, *The Kingdom of Kongo*, Oxford, 1985.

Iselin, Regula, 'Reading Pictures: On the Value of the Copperplates in the *Beschryvinghe* of Pieter de Marees (1602) as Source Material for Ethnohistorical Research', *History in Africa*, 21, 1994, pp. 147–70.

Israel, Jonathan I., *Dutch Primacy in World Trade, 1585–1740*, Oxford, 1989.

——, 'The Economic Contribution of the Dutch Sephardhi Jewry to Holland's Golden Age, 1593–1713', in Jonathan Israel, *Empires and Entrepots: the Dutch, the Spanish Monarchy, and the Jews, 1585–1713*, London, 1990, pp. 19–22.

IJzermann, J. W., *Journal van de Reis naar Zuid-Amerika (1598–1601) door Hendrick Ottsen*, 's-Gravenhage, 1918.

——, *Cornelis Buysero te Bantam, 1616–1618*, 's-Gravenhage, 1923.

——, *De Reis om de Wereld door Oliver van Noort (1598–1601),* 2 vols, 's-Gravenhage, 1926.

Jones, Adam, 'Double Dutch: A Survey of Seventeenth-Century German Sources for West African History', *History in Africa*, 9, 1982, pp. 140–53.

——, *German Sources for West African History 1599–1669*, Wiesbaden, 1983.

——, *Brandenburg Sources for West African History, 1680–1700*, Stuttgart, 1985.

——, 'A Critique of Editorial and Quasi-Editorial Work on pre–1885 European Sources for Sub-Saharan Africa, 1960–1986', *Paideuma*, 33, 1987, pp. 95–106.

——, *Raw, Medium, Well Done: A Critical Review of Editorial and Quasi-Editorial Work on Pre–1885 European Sources for Sub-Saharan Africa, 1960–1988*, Madison, African Studies Program, University of Wisconsin-Madison, 1987.

——, 'Decompiling Dapper: A Preliminary Search for Evidence, *History in Africa*, 17, 1990, pp. 171–209.

——, *Zur Quellenproblematik des Geschichte Westafrikas, 1450–1900*, Stuttgart, 1990.

——, 'Drink Deep, or Taste Not: Thoughts on the Use of Early European Records in the Study of African Material Culture', *History in Africa*, 21, 1994, pp. 349–70.

——, *West Africa in the Mid-Seventeenth Century: An Anonymous Dutch Manuscript*, Atlanta, African Studies Association, 1995.

Klein, P. W., *De Trippen in de 17e Eeuw: Een Studie over het Ondernemersgedrag op de Hollandse Stapelmarkt*. Assen, 1965.

L'Hour, Michel, *et al.*, *Le Mauritius: la mémoire engloutie*, Paris, 1989.

Lanwehr, John, *VOC: A Bibliography of Publications Relating to the Dutch East India Company, 1602–1800*, Utrecht, 1991.

MacGaffey, Wyatt and Michael D. Harris, *Astonishment and Power: The Eyes of Understanding Kongo Mnkisi*, Washington DC, 1993.

Martin, Phyllis M., *The External Trade of the Loango Coast, 1576–1870*, Oxford, 1972.

——, 'Power, Cloth, and Currency on the Loango Coast', *Muntu*, 7, 1987, pp. 135–47.

Mauny, Raymond, 'Notes d'histoire sur Rufisque, *Notes africaines*, 46, 1950, pp. 47–9.

Miller, Joseph C., *Kings and Kingsmen: Early Mbundu States in Angola*, Oxford, 1976.

——, *Way of Death: Merchant Capitalism and the Angolan Slave Trade, 1730–1830*, Madison, Wisconsin, 1988.

Miracle, Marvin, *Maize in Tropical Africa*, Madison, Wisconsin, 1966.

Moreland, W. H., 'Pieter van den Broecke at Surat, 1620–29, *Journal of Indian History*, 10, 1931, pp. 235–50; and 11, 1931, pp. 1–16 and 203–18.

Müller, Wilhelm Johann. See Jones, 1983

Naber, S. P. L'Honoré, *Pieter de Marees, Beschryvinghe ende Historische verhael, van het Gout Koninckrijck van Gunea*, 's-Gravenhage, 1912.

——, *Toortse der Zee-Vaert door Dierick Ruiters (1623)* and *Samuel Brun's Schiffarten (1624)* [bound in one volume], 's-Gravenhage, 1913.

Narain, Brij and Sri Ram Sharma, trans. and eds, *A Contemporary Dutch Chronicle of Mughal India*, Calcutta, 1957.

Ottsen, Hendrick. See IJzerman, 1912.

Patterson, K. David, *The Northern Gabon Coast to 1875*, Oxford, 1975.

Pechuel-Loesche, Eduard, *Die Loango-Expedition ausgesandt von der Deutschen ...*, Leipzig, 1882.

Perrot, Claude-Hélène, 'Semallies et moissons dans la région d'Assine vers 1700', *Journal des africanistas*, 60, 1990, pp. 9–25.

Postma, Johannes M., *The Dutch in the Atlantic Slave Trade, 1600–1815*, New York, 1990.

Posthumus, N. W., *Inquiry Into the History of Prices in Holland*, 2 vols, Leiden, 1946.

Ratelband, K., ed., *Reizen naar West-Afrika van Pieter van den Broecke, 1605–1614*, 's-Gravenhage, 1950.

——, *Vijf dagregisters van het kasteel Sao Jorge da Mina (Elmina) aan de Goudkust (1645–1647) door Jacob Ruychaver en Jacob van der Wel*, 's-Gravenhage, 1953.

Ravenstein, E. G., ed., *The Strange Adventures of Andrew Battel in Angola and the Adjoining Regions*, London, Hakluyt Society, 1st series, 1901; reprinted Nendelen, 1967.

Reesse, J. J., *De suikerhandel van Amsterdam het begin der 17e eeuw tot 1813*, Haarlem, 1908.

Rossel, Gerda, *Taxonomic-Linguistic Study of Plantain in Africa*, Leiden, CNWS, 1998.

Ruiters, Dierick. See Naber, 1913.

Schwartz, Stuart B., *Sugar Plantations in the Formation of Brazilian Society*, Cambridge, 1985.

Steensgaard, Neils, 'The Companies as a Specific Institution in the History of European Expansion', in Leonard Blussé and Femme Gaastra, eds, *Companies and Trade: Essays on Overseas Trading Companies during the Ancien Régime*, Leiden, 1981, pp. 245–64.

Swartenbroeckx, Pierre, *Dictionnaire Kikongo et Kituba-Français*, Bandundu: CEEBA, 1973.

Thilmans, Guy, and De Moraes, Nize Izabel, 'Dencha Four, souverain du Baol (XVIIe siècle)', *Bulletin de l'I.F.A.N.*, sér. B, 36, 4, 1974, pp. 691–713.

——, 'Les Passages à la Petite Côte de Pieter van den Broecke (1606–1609)', *Bulletin de l'I.F.A.N.*, sér.B, 39, 3, 1977, pp. 471–92.

Thom, H. B., *Journal of Jan van Riebeeck*. Vol. I., Cape Town, 1952.

Thornton, John K., 'New Light on Cavazzi's Seventeenth-Century Description of Kongo', *History in Africa*, 6, 1979, pp. 253–64.

——, *The Kingdom of Kongo: Civil War and Transition, 1641–1718*, Madison, Wisconsin, 1983.

——, 'The Development of an African Catholic Church in the Kingdom of Kongo, 1491–1750'. *Journal of African History*, 25, 1 (1984), pp. 147–67.

——, 'The Art of War in Angola, 1575–1680', *Comparative Studies in Society and History*, 30, 1988, pp. 360–78.

——, *Africa and Africans in the Making of the Atlantic World, 1400–1680*, Cambridge, 1992.

Tilleman, Erick. See Winsnes, 1994

Towerson, William. See Blake, 1967

Ulsheimer, Andreas Josua. See Jones, 1983

Unger, Richard W., *Dutch Shipbuilding before 1800: Ships and Guilds*, Assen, 1978.

Unger, W. S., 'Nieuwe gegevens betreffende het begin der vaart op Guinea', *Economisch-historisch Jaarboek*, 21, 1940, pp. 194–217.

Van Brakel, S., *De Hollandsche Handelscompagnieën der Zeventiende Eeuw*, 's-Gravenhage, 1908.

Van Dantzig, Albert and Adam Jones, eds and trans., *Pieter de Marees, Description and Historical Account of the Gold Kingdom of Guinea (1602)*, Oxford, 1987.

Van de Wall, V. I, *Nederlandsche Oudheden in de Molukken*, 's-Gravenhage, 1928.

Van den Boogaart, Ernst, 'Books on Black Africa: The Dutch Publications and their Owners in the Seventeenth Century', *Paideuma*, 33, 1987, pp. 115–26.

——, 'The Trade between Western Africa and the Atlantic World, 1600–90: Estimates of Trends in Composition and Value', *Journal of African History*, 33, 2, 1992, pp. 369–85.

Van den Broecke, Pieter. See Coolhaas, 1962–3; Ratelband, 1950; Thilmans and De Moraes, 1977

Van Deursen, A. Th., *Resolutiën der Staten-Generaal, 1600–1670, Part I, 1610–1612*, 's-Gravenhage, 1971.

Van Gelder, J. G., 'Dateering van Frans Hals' portret van P. v. d. Broecke', *Oud Holland*, 60, 1938, 154.

Van Noort, Oliver. See IJzerman, 1926

Vansina, Jan, 'The Bells of Kings', *Journal of African History*, 10, 1969, pp. 187–97.

——, 'Finding Food and the History of Precolonial Equatorial Africa: A Plea', *African Economic History*, 7, 1979, pp. 9–20.

——, *Paths in the Rainforests: Towards a History of Political Tradition in Equatorial Africa*, Madison, Wisconsin, 1988.

Van Wassenaer, Nicholaas, *Historisch verhael aller ghedenckweerdiger geschiedenissen* ..., Amsterdam, 1624–7.

Vogt, John, *Portuguese Rule of the Gold Coast, 1469–1682*, Athens, Georgia, 1979.

Webb, James L. A., *Desert Frontier: Ecological and Economic Change along the Western Sahel, 1600–1850*, Madison, Wisconsin, 1995.

Wigboldus, Jouke S., 'De oudste Indonesische maïscultuur', in F. van Anrooy, *et al.*, *Between People and Statistics: Essays on Modern Indonesian History*, 's-Gravenhage, 1979.

Winsnes, Selena Axelrod, trans. and ed. *Erick Tilleman, En Kort of Engoldig Enfoldig Beretning om det Landskab Guinea of dets Beskaffenhed*, Madison, African Studies Program, University of Wisconsin-Madison, 1994.

INDEXES

INDEX OF PERSONS

Note that this index uses just one spelling of the names that Van den Broecke recorded in his manuscript in often inconsistent ways. Dutch naming traditions are briefly described above, on pp. 19–20. Note also that this index is alphabetized using conventional English, rather than Dutch, rules.

INDEX OF PLACES

Note that this index uses modern names of toponyms, rather than the historic but often inconsistent spellings Van den Broecke used in his manuscript.

INDEX OF SELECT SUBJECTS

Note the following general listings: ANIMALS, PLANTS, and TRADE COMMODITIES.